PRAISE FOR *CHURCH*

"As two hearts resonated on the way to En
of our resurrected Lord Jesus Christ, your heart will resonate to the teaching and
testimonies of this amazing book. It will resonate in the heart of the person next
to you and the next generation. Don't miss the opportunity to be part of heaven's
melody, resonating in God's heart!"

—Vladimir Cizmanski, *Pastor*, Montenegro

"It's 11:15 pm on Easter night 2014, and I just finished reading *Church on
Fire*. It is an exciting growth prescription for every church and person that will
read it. Fred's use of personal experiences, along with an easy-read writing style,
adds to the powerful message and its proof of success."

—Jim Doss, *CEO/Chairman*, Structural Concepts Corporation

"Once again, Fred Hartley has given us a book not only filled with a passion
for revival and awakening, but with practical tools on how to cooperate with
God in the process. God is stirring across our land. *Church on Fire* is not only
the book we need, but the movement we need! May God use it to continue to
awaken and ignite His sleeping church with His presence."

—Bill Elliff, *Pastor*, The Summit Church
Little Rock, Arkansas

"If you are looking for a practical game plan to see the fires of prayer ignited
in your church, then *Church on Fire* is a book you must read. Every time my
friend, Fred Hartley, writes a book, I am stretched and inspired in my pursuit of
the manifest presence of God. In *Church on Fire*, he inspired me to long for the
fire of God's presence for my whole faith family as well. It will not only stretch
and inspire your prayer life, but it also lays out a practical plan to see the power
of prayer unleashed in your church body. Every pastor should read this book."

—Chip Henderson, *Pastor*, Pinelake Church, Jackson, Mississippi

"Fred Hartley provides us with a tool to help us turn things around in our
own hearts and our nation – a 31-day prayer guide that is filled with how-tos,
stories of victory, scriptures to live by and more! Your prayer life WILL change
if you commit yourself to walk through 31 days of prayer."

—Os Hillman, *President*, Marketplace Leaders

"I encountered the teachings of Fred Hartley at a conference in Bethlehem in 2012. I never thought that his teaching would change my sleeping schedule and provoke me to wake up at 4 am every morning in order to spend time with God. This book elaborates the teachings of that conference. It will challenge congregations to encounter Christ and serve Him from a Spirit-filled and Spirit-saturated perspective. Be careful, it will change your life!"

—Yohanna Katanacho, *Academic Dean*
Bethlehem Bible College and Galilee Bible College

"I shout 'Hallelujah!' When this book is published, our church will be the first to use it. If you are bored and tired of the routine and long for the manifest presence of God, read this book. Then read this book with your leadership teams."

—Ron Mitchell, *Pastor,* Rancho Murieta Community Church

"In our missionary community, we are asking, 'Lord, teach us to pray.' *Church on Fire* has been the single most encouraging and helpful book to us in this season of relearning to pray and refocusing our commitment to the Lord and His glory over the nations."

—Burt Plaster, *President*, WEC International

"Thirty-one days. Thirty-one challenges. Hundreds of churches ignited by God's presence. Of this I am certain. With *Church on Fire*, Fred Hartley takes the powerful principles of personal revival from his masterful God on Fire and applies them where they are so desperately needed – the local church. The book's day-by-day approach never lets the reader go, never stops leading onto hallowed ground."

—Michael Scales, *President*
Nyack College & Alliance Theological Seminary

"*Church on Fire* will take you and your church into experiencing the manifest presence of Christ. If that sounds as exciting to you as it does to me, then pick up this book and get started!"

—Jimmy Seibert, *President*, Antioch Ministries International
Senior Pastor, Antioch Community Church, Waco, Texas

"*Church on Fire* is deeply inspirational to the individual, the local church, and the church worldwide. Its strength comes from Fred knowing, loving and serving peoples in many countries. It plants hope for change that comes from encountering Christ Himself and what He can do though prayer. It is filled with profound thoughts and slogans, and moves from the personal to the corporate to the leadership to the world. Your prayer life will never be the same after reading it."

—Imad Shehadeh, *President*, Jordan Evangelical Theological Seminary

"*God on Fire* is one of my favorite books, as it is one of the few books I have read multiple times. *Church on Fire* will accompany that book as a great tool and practical resource to seek the Lord. I am eager to share it with my many friends. I highly recommend it to you, but be ready for God to do a work in your heart!"

—Dann Spader, *Founder*, Sonlife Ministries

"Fred Hartley over the years has produced some of the best helps on prayer for the local church. The book, *Church on Fire*, is his best. Fred Hartley has well received a Word to help in having a praying church. I rank it as one of the best I have ever read and heartily recommend it."

—Terry Teykl, *Founder*, Pray for Renewal Ministries

"Have you ever been to the 'upper room' in the book of Acts? Ever wonder what it was like — the smell in the air, the sound of the prayers, and the fury of the Holy Spirit? Well, *Church on Fire* will take you there. As the third book in the *On Fire* series, Hartley turns his attention to the praying mission of the larger church — yes, that includes us all. In classic Hartley style, the book cuts quick and deep and leaves no soul in its comfort zone. Whether it is the direct challenge to pastors to answer the question of what God is doing versus what they are doing or the call for less prayer meetings and more receiving meetings or asking what separates the church from the sports bar down the street or the blunt truth that only prayer meetings reach people not board meetings or planning meetings, *Church on Fire* never backs down from relentlessly asking how the manifest presence of Christ is revealing itself in the church and its people. Hartley knows how to be practical and *Church on Fire* has a handbook feel with its step by step walk through issues like repentance and contrition or the beautiful power of simply agreeing in prayer with your spouse. *Church on Fire?* More like Church engulfed!"

—John Towriss, *Principal*, Envoy Strategy Group

"I love the heartbeat of Fred Hartley. Single-minded passion to see God move, the kind Fred demonstrates, is desperately needed in the church. This guide will help you walk your leaders through a step-by-step process to whet their appetites for the presence of God. May it bear fruit that remains!"

—Steven W. Smith, *Professor of Communication*
Southwestern Baptist Theological Seminary

"*Church on Fire* is an amazing follow-up to Fred Hartley's book, *God on Fire.* It gives pastors and leaders a great tool that will help bring real transformation to their congregations. This book provides practical answers and learning exercises that will train people in the school of prayer and passion for Jesus. I strongly recommend *Church on Fire* to pastors and churches."

—Ron Walborn, *Dean*, Alliance Theological Seminary

"Fred Hartley cuts right to the heart and provides us with a road map to get the church back on track and to experience His presence. If you are bold enough to take this adventure, your life will never be the same."

—Bill Welte, *President/CEO* America's Keswick

"Fred Hartley has written a practical guide for those who are interested in deepening their prayer life and experiencing the manifest presence of Christ among his people. And that should be all of us! Everyone who longs for Christ's presence and power to be manifest in the church will profit."

—Daniel Wetzel, *Vice President,* The Christian and Missionary Alliance

CHURCH
ON
FIRE

A **31-Day Adventure** to Welcome
the Manifest Presence of Christ

Fred A. Hartley, III

PUBLICATIONS
Fort Washington, PA 19034

Church on Fire
Published by CLC Publications

U.S.A.
P.O. Box 1449, Fort Washington, PA 19034

UNITED KINGDOM
CLC International (UK)
51 The Dean, Alresford, Hampshire, SO24 9BJ

Printed in the United States of America

ISBN-10 (paperback): 1-61958-180-9
ISBN-13 (paperback): 978-1-61958-180-7
ISBN-13 (e-book): 978-1-61958-181-4

DEDICATION

To my dear friends and ministry partners
in Jerusalem and throughout the Holy Land:
Jack and Madleine Sara
Mazen and Randa Nasrawi
Suhail and Lina Dabbagh
Magdy and Rima Anwar
Bassem and Jesura Adranly
Simone and Fatulla Ratidi
Yohanna and Dina Katanacho,
Sandy, Shukry, Christine, Monica and David,
who are rebuilding the flame holder of the upper room today.
I love you and honor you.
It is one of the greatest privileges of my life
to link arms with you as you experience the reality of
church on fire!

CONTENTS

INTRODUCTION

When Christ built His church, He built a praying church.
Is your church a praying church?
When Jesus made disciples, He made praying disciples.
What kind of disciples are you making?
The size of your ministry is determined by the size of your prayer life.
For what are you asking God?
The size of your prayer life is revealed by the size of your answers to prayer.
What size answers are you receiving?
God set the early church on fire with the manifest presence of Christ.
Is God setting your church on fire?

This book defines church the way Jesus defined church—as a house of prayer for all nations on fire with the manifest presence of Christ.

Two years ago my phone rang on a Sunday afternoon. "My name is Jack Sara, pastor of the only evangelical church in the old city of Jerusalem," the man calling explained. "Several of us pastors here in Jerusalem have heard about the College of Prayer. We are desperate for God. We want to invite you to bring the College of Prayer to our land. If you are ever in Jerusalem, we would love to meet with you."

"Ever in Jerusalem?" I laughed. "I'll be there Tuesday!" I explained to Jack that while I had never previously been to Israel, after three years of planning, I would arrive that week with a team for a Holy Land prayer trip. He and I both marveled at the miraculous timing of his phone call.

Two days later I was sitting with a dozen pastors and leaders from Israel and Palestine, and these leaders invited the College of Prayer to return to Israel a month later to help the church in the Holy Land to experience a fresh encounter with Christ and help them become a praying church. I explained to them that while I was honored to be invited to serve them in any way I could, there was no way that I could possibly return that year.

"We are desperate for God," they explained. "We can't wait until next year. We can't even wait six months. The church in the Holy Land needs a genuine move of the Holy Spirit. We need a breakthrough. We need you to return next month to train us to reach a lost world through a revived church." Needless to say, their desperation for God was impressive.

My wife and I fell in love with this group immediately. Our initial meeting with these leaders was the beginning of an ongoing kingdom partnership with some very special people. I have had the privilege of serving both local and regional churches all over the world through the College of Prayer, but the wholehearted earnestness and zeal of the church in the Holy Land is truly unique.

Since then my team and I have returned twice each year to serve the church in Israel. The biblical principles I have taught them are the same principles that are contained in this book. They are the very same principles that Jesus first taught right there in Israel and Palestine two thousand years ago. They are the principles that have shaped my local church in metro Atlanta and have been used to build Christ-exalting, nation-reaching, God-encountering churches in forty-one other countries of the world through the College of Prayer.

For the next thirty-one days, it will be my honor to stand with you in the same way I stand with the precious believers in Jerusalem. You will discover that not every day of our six-week adventure is of equal length, but each day is, nevertheless, of equal value. Some days require more reading, some more time in reflection. Take your time to fully engage with both the readings and the reflection questions. These kingdom principles will help you not only to build a praying church but will empower you to reach a lost world through a revived church.

If you have a gnawing hunger deep down in your belly for more of Christ,

if you want to see marriages healed,

if you want your children to see dramatic answers to specific prayers,

if you want to see people in your church and in your neighborhood set free from demonic bondages and self-destructive behavior,

if you want physical and emotional healings to be a daily occurrence,

if you want to see every member in your church experience firsthand the joy of leading a neighbor to Christ, then I can assure you that you are in the right place!

And if you are a pastor who is putting in seventy-plus hours a week with little to show for it,

if you have seen modest results but know that there is much more where those came from,

if you are tired of spending all your energies just keeping the church machinery moving,

if you have been working too hard and praying too little,

if you are ready to shift from focusing on what you do at church to what God does,

if you want to build a praying church and make upper-room, God-encountering disciples,

if you want to activate and utilize the revelatory gifts in your life and in your church family,

if you want to equip your people to effectively reach their neighbors and the nations,

then our thirty-one-day adventure has far-reaching potential both for you and your church family.

Welcome to *church on fire*!

Now It's Your Turn: Action Steps

This book is intentionally called a thirty-one-day adventure because it is designed to take you places. This is not simply reading material or busy work; through it you will have an opportunity to move forward in your journey with Jesus. As you read it, you will be invited to encounter the manifest presence of Christ on a personal level; and as a gatekeeper in your local church, you will have an opportunity to include others with you in the adventure. Each week specific action steps are included just for your benefit.

Questions for Small Groups

Small group questions have been provided for each week of this adventure as well. If you lead a small group, select the questions that you would like to use from the list included after each week's adventure.

Advice for Pastors

Although this book has been written for ministry leaders of all kinds, it is particularly applicable to pastors. Since you are a leader, and since leaders like to know where they are going, you may want to look ahead before reading this book at the "Advice for Pastors" section at the end of each week's adventure.

Be blessed as you journey toward *church on fire*!

GET READY FOR FIRE

On the surface, church is what we do. It is the gathering together of Christ followers in order for us to love God, love each other and love our neighbors for Jesus' sake. Churches come in various shapes and sizes, but no matter how we slice it, our gathering is our effort to engage with God and His people.

Fire, on the other hand, is what God does. It is the initiative of the invisible God to demonstrate His supernatural power in tangible ways that we can all understand. Answers to prayer, physical healings, saved marriages, deliverance from evil strongholds, dramatic conversions and changed lives are all examples of fire. It is what happens when God comes to church. Point-blank, fire is the manifest presence of Christ.

Church on fire is what happens when what we do and what God does slam together. It is church the way God intended—where we become even more conscious of His presence among us than we are conscious of those with whom we gather.

Fire is what sets apart the church from the sports bar or the fitness center down the street. Any organization on earth can show what people can do; only the church can show what Christ can do. For this reason, whenever God is about to send the fire of His manifest presence, He always prepares His people in advance.

Welcome to an adventure of a lifetime. Week one is your get-ready-for-the-fire week, in which you will rebuild your own heart to seek after Christ. I hope that you are not only ready and eager—I also hope that you will bring others with you on this journey. In many ways the effectiveness of your entire thirty-one-day adventure depends on how thoroughly you allow Christ to get you ready during this first week. An Olympic gold medalist wins the center platform at the awards ceremony, not just at the sporting event, but in the months of preparation leading up to it. For the next thirty-one days, beginning with week one, we will aim to encounter the manifest presence of Christ and experience firsthand *church on fire*.

Day 1

START ASKING

If you want fire, you need to ask for it. God loves to come to where He is invited. He loves to manifest the reality of His flaming presence when we ask Him to do it. The prophet Elijah lowered the tip of his sword and drew a line in the sand one day as he defined a universal kingdom principle, one not only for the believers in his day but for your church and mine.

"The god who answers by fire—he is God" (1 Kings 18:24).

God was the God who answered by fire in Elijah's day, and He is just as much the God who answers by fire in our day. The prophet Elijah proceeded to pray a remarkably simple prayer: "O LORD, God of Abraham, Isaac and Israel, let it be known today that you are God in Israel and that I am your servant and have done all these things at your command. Answer me, O LORD, answer me so these people will know that you, O LORD, are God, and that you are turning their hearts back again" (1 Kings 18:36–37). More than preaching this principle, Elijah practiced what he preached. He didn't simply believe *in* fire, he believed *for* fire. He asked, and he received.

Perhaps the most shocking part of this prayer is that Elijah never specifically asked for fire. With everything riding on the outcome of his prayer, we would have expected him to pray for fire explicitly, but he never did—not for literal fire. What he requested was the manifest presence of God: "Let it be known today that you are God in Israel . . . so these people will know that you, O LORD, are God." Elijah prayed for the manifest presence of God and the effect that the manifest presence of God would have on the people—that they would know that God was "turning their hearts back again."

Not only did fire fall that day, but hearts and lives were turned back to the Lord.

Do you want the fire of God's manifest presence to fall again in your church? Are you asking God for fire?

Headline News from Jerusalem

Headline News provides breaking news from the Middle East. Allow me to share with you a story of good news that you may not have heard from Headline News, CNN or any other news outlet.

I stood in the middle of the only evangelical church in the old city of Jerusalem on a Sunday in August 2013, and I was thoroughly overwhelmed as the atmosphere exuded the presence of Christ. Small groups of believers were huddled together all around me in God-encountering prayer and worship. Some knelt. Some stood. Many wept as spontaneous prayers of repentance rose from around the room. We gathered that day in the building where they worship every Sunday, just off the Via Dolorosa, only a couple hundred meters or so from the place where many believe Jesus died. On this particular day these dear believers were wholeheartedly crying out to God, asking Him to make them a house of prayer for all nations and to empower them again to build an upper-room, "God-encountering prayer meeting" in their city. As I stood among them, I too wept tears of overwhelming gratitude.

I knew that I was standing on holy ground—smack dab in the middle of Jerusalem, the crossroads of civilization. Christ was pouring into these people His Holy Spirit, activating the gifts of His Spirit, clothing the church with power so He could thrust its members out to be His witnesses right there in Jerusalem. He would use them to win many to faith in Christ—Catholics, Armenians, Muslims, Orthodox and Jews. This church was alive—alive in prayer, alive to God's manifest presence and alive to fulfill the purpose of Christ in its generation. I shook my head in wonder as God moved among its people. Christ was rebuilding the upper-room, God-encountering prayer meeting in the same city in which He had built the very first upper-room prayer gathering.

Of all the churches the College of Prayer has served around the world, I know of none more alive in worship, more fervent in prayer, more desperate for Christ, more active in the revelatory gifts and more effective at reaching lost people for Christ than this congregation in Jerusalem. Many pastors throughout Israel and Palestine tell me that this evangelical church within the Old City is probably the only church in the land that is effectively seeing significant numbers from the majority group of Palestinian people come to faith in Christ. It is no wonder that they are so fruitful in soul winning, since they are doing church ministry the way Jesus told them to do it.

This particular move of God on this Sunday morning in this strategic location did not happen in a vacuum. It was part of a sustained move of God that had been developing over many years. God had prepared these people to ask, and they had been asking fervently. Now they are receiving, and they are receiving fully. The God who answers by fire is answering the prayers of these dear believers today.

Lord, Teach Us to Pray

I didn't always know how to receive fire, let alone lead others into the fire of Christ's manifest presence. When I finished graduate school, I began serving as pastor of my first church. After less than a year in my new ministry, I woke up in the middle of one night with severe chest pains. I could hardly breathe. I thought I was dying. My wife dialed 911. The rescue unit came and rushed me to the hospital. I was diagnosed with two problems: heart fibrillation and severe indigestion. My heart was beating so fast that it was almost vibrating, but it was not effectively pumping blood through my body. The indigestion was caused by the onion rings and Coke I'd had at midnight. Not a good combination! My church had tripled in size, though that's not saying much, as we had grown from twenty-three members to seventy-five. My cardiologist, however, told me that I was suffering from battle fatigue and that unless I wanted to die before I turned thirty, I needed to slow down. God told me that I was working too hard and praying too little.

I knew that I needed to learn to pray, so I registered for a revival-prayer conference with J. Edwin Orr and Armin Gesswein. On separate days I took both men out for lunch. I felt like a little bird with my mouth wide open, waiting to eat up any morsels that these godly men dropped in my direction. This began a lifelong relationship with both men, particularly with Armin Gesswein.

Armin had been the first prayer leader at Billy Graham's crusades. When Billy preached in Los Angeles and led so many Hollywood movie stars to Christ in 1949, he preached in one tent to ten thousand people, while Armin Gesswein simultaneously led a prayer meeting in a separate tent with two thousand intercessors. Over the years Armin had mentored many leaders in prayer, including Bill Bright, Chuck Smith, Ray Ortlund, Ted Engstrom, Robert Schuller and scores of others.

As he and I ate lunch together, Armin stuck out his long, bony finger over his large bowl of romaine lettuce and said to me with a half smile,

"If you want to learn to pray, you need to pray." He let that statement sink in and then added, "Start where the disciples started with the short and simple prayer, 'Lord, teach us to pray'" (Luke 11:1). "It may be the shortest prayer you'll ever pray," he added, "only five words—but it's the most important prayer you'll ever pray." Over the next seventeen years, I would hear Armin say that same thing at least a hundred times. "Once God teaches you to pray," he added as we finished lunch, "you can receive from Him anything He wants you to have."

I returned to my church south of Miami, Florida, with a new prayer: "Lord, teach us to pray." I prayed it forcefully, and I prayed it often. I taught my church leaders and my entire congregation to pray it. I have now taught literally millions of believers around the world to pray these five words.

"Lord, teach us to pray" is a prayer that God loves to hear. It's as if when He hears these five words from a hungry heart, He turns His head to listen.

"Lord, teach us to pray" is asking the right person the right question—the question He has been waiting to hear. The fact is that none of us knows how to pray as we ought (see Rom. 8:26). There are not two groups of people in the world—those who don't know how to pray as they ought and those who do. There are only those who don't know how to pray as they ought and those who think they do, and the latter group is wrong. We don't even start praying correctly until we admit that we don't know how to pray correctly and, more specifically, until we ask God for help. No one can teach us to pray the way God can.

"Lord, teach us to pray" does not say, "Lord, teach us about prayer." It specifically asks God to activate us to true prayer.

"Lord, teach us to pray" is a corporate prayer request. Many of us have privatized prayer. Of course, prayer initially rises from us as individuals, but the thrust of this five-word prayer of the disciples, and the thrust of this book, is the same as the New Testament thrust of corporate prayer. The "us" of "Lord, teach us to pray" is the reason Jesus called for a house of prayer and not for individual apartments. It's the reason we are called a royal priesthood and not just a bunch of private priests. This is why Jesus said, "Where two or three come together in my name, there am I with them" (Matt. 18:20). Christ wants us to come together, to come together in corporate prayer. He wants our gatherings to be full of prayer so that we can be full of His presence. This is the essence of *church on fire*.

Now It's Your Turn: Day 1 Action Step

"Lord, teach us to pray" is a spark that lights the flame of *church on fire*. These five words are not magic, but they are biblical. You and your church family will want to pray them regularly, even daily. As you do, God will indeed teach you to pray and open up to you a whole new world. Since fire is God's work, not yours, ask Him today to send fire as you pray the following biblical promises. Take your time. Read each verse carefully. Ask God to put in your spirit an ever-increasing desire to pray.

The God who answers by fire—he is God. (1 Kings 18:24)

One day Jesus was praying in a certain place. When he finished, one of his disciples said to him, "Lord, teach us to pray, just as John taught his disciples." (Luke 11:1)

I say to you: Ask and it will be given to you; seek and you will find; knock and the door will be opened to you. For everyone who asks receives; he who seeks finds; and to him who knocks, the door will be opened. (11:9–10)

If you then, though you are evil, know how to give good gifts to your children, how much more will your Father in heaven give the Holy Spirit to those who ask him! (11:13)

Seek the LORD while he may be found; call on him while he is near. (Isa. 55:6)

Draw near to God and He will draw near to you. (James 4:8, NASB)

Without faith it is impossible to please God, because anyone who comes to him must believe that he exists and that he rewards those who earnestly seek him. (Heb. 11:6)

Lord Jesus, what You are teaching me today is _____

_____

Lord Jesus, the action step that I will take is _____

_____

Day 2

GET HUNGRY

Health and hunger go hand in hand. This principle is true in both the physical and spiritual realms. When I was in high school, my mother knew that if I lost my appetite, it was for only one of two possible reasons: I was either sick, or I was in love! When we lose our appetite for Christ, it means that we are either spiritually sick, or we are in love with something other than Christ. Spiritual health and spiritual hunger are inseparably linked.

The hungrier we are, the healthier we are, and the hungrier we are, the better we pray. Hunger for God is always part of the get-ready-for-revival preparatory work of God. "Hunger is the best cook," the great Reformer Martin Luther said.[1] Luther knew from experience what he was talking about.

Hunger for God is itself the work of God. The Bible says that no one seeks after God (see Rom. 3:11). This means that when we start to seek God, it is always because God sounded the appetite alarm within us. When God creates hunger for Himself in one person, it is often an indicator that God is creating a similar hunger for Himself within others around that person as well. If you and your people have a gnawing pain in the pit of your stomach to encounter more of Christ, you may be closer to a breakthrough than you think.

Hunger and Desperation

I have never met anyone hungrier for God than Moise Guindo, president of the Christian and Missionary Alliance church in Mali, West Africa. He led seven hundred churches with a total of seventy thousand baptized believers.[2] When I first met him, he had been sitting on his moped at a fork in a dirt road on the edge of the Sahara Desert, eagerly awaiting our arrival, for two hours. He escorted us to the best hotel in town, which had dirt floors, no air-conditioning, no running water and no toilet. After we finished all the African protocol greetings, we sat down kneecap to kneecap. Moise took my hands, looked me straight in the eyes and with the deepest sincerity I had ever felt, simply said, "We need God!"

He dropped to his knees and said with tears, "I cannot lead these people unless the Holy Spirit comes and manifests His presence among us."

As we held hands, he wept. His tears hit the dirt floor, and to this day I can still see the darkened spots that his tears made on the ground. The level of desperation in his soul was palpable. I can still feel the intensity, sincerity, humility and guilelessness of his heart. I have never before nor since sensed anything like it. I breathed a prayer: "Lord, You owe this man revival."[3] I knew that God was about to do something extraordinary, and He did. That week I witnessed an extraordinary move of the Holy Spirit among the massive group of several hundred pastors. I saw high worship, deep repentance, confession of sin, breaking of demonic strongholds, receiving of the infilling of the Holy Spirit and empowerment for ministry before the pastors returned to their assignments throughout their country.

On one occasion that week, we engaged in eight hours of nonstop repentance. I will never forget watching grown men weep like school children as they humbled themselves in the presence of a holy God. We heard every imaginable sin confessed that day. Don't think that this was merely an emotional or superficial response; it was deep, life changing and long lasting. When my team returned two years later, those same pastors were still walking in victory and freedom.

The Hourglass Vision

You may be thinking, *I'm not as desperate for the Lord as Moise was.* Not so fast. Before you underestimate your hunger and desperation for God, you need to realize that there are two doorways to desperation, and both doorways are equally valid:

- The front door to desperation = a pitiful present
- The back door to desperation = a preferred future

Many churches enter into desperation through the front door of a pitiful present. Things are so bad in their circumstances that unless God breaks through, they are doomed to utter failure. Churches in the Middle East, Africa, China and Southeast Asia, as well as parts of Latin America, are so overwhelmed by the external forces of religious oppression or the internal forces of sin, selfishness and immorality that they have entered into desperation for God by the front door.

Churches in North America, Europe, Australia and other well-off parts of the world, however, are entering desperation through the back door. They see a preferred future—they recognize that there is far more that God has for them than what they are currently experiencing. The church in South Korea has perhaps the most vibrant prayer movement on earth today. Its people pray with great zeal, urgency and intensity. It is also the fastest-growing missionary church on earth. Their desperation for God is not because of a pitiful present but rather a preferred future—they see more that God wants to do through them.

My friend Chip Henderson is lead pastor of the largest church in Mississippi. He is in the midst of transforming his church into a praying church. He and his leadership team are desperate for God, not because things are going poorly but because they have a vision for so much more that they want from God.

Both doors to desperation bring us to the same conclusion: we do not have what it takes within ourselves to meet the challenges and opportunities in front of us. God alone has what it takes. Prayer is the way we access God's resources.

One day as I was praying, I saw a most disturbing picture. I saw an hourglass. The bottom of the glass represented the vast needs of people, and I began to weep over the wounds of hurting, lost people and over the lukewarm church that seemed impotent to meet their needs. The top of the hourglass represented God's endless resources—all His redemptive provision. I became even more overwhelmed. "What can I do to open up the constriction in the middle of the glass to get the unlimited redemptive resources of God at the top down more quickly to meet the needs of the people on the bottom?" I asked God. "Why is God not flowing faster to meet the needs of the people? Why is the middle of the hourglass so constricted?" The Lord answered me, "The constriction in the middle is the lack of prayer in the church." I wept and wept.

I have seen this hourglass picture while praying dozens of times since then. Each time my burden of desperation grows greater. The bottom of the glass is a picture of the front door to desperation, representing the overwhelming needs of people. The top of the hourglass is a picture of the back door to desperation, representing the resources and the redemption of Christ. Both the top and the bottom of the glass, both the front and the back door, move us to want to cry out in desperation for the redemptive resources of God to more rapidly meet the needs of hurting, lost people around us.

At the College of Prayer, we have discovered that every church around the world currently experiencing the fire of the manifest presence of Christ has one thing in common: desperation. The College of Prayer is now serving fifteen of the twenty most persecuted churches on earth. The members of each of these churches know that they have no hope of accomplishing anything for Christ in their country unless they experience the supernatural power of the manifest presence of Christ. Churches in China, the Middle East and across North Africa don't need to be told to pray. They are desperate and know that their lives depend on prayer. For them it is not an option—it is their lifeline.

Now It's Your Turn: Day 2 Action Step

If you are hungry, pray your hunger away. If you are not hungry, repent and ask God to sound your appetite alarm. These verses may help you to express your desperation to God. Take time to read each verse slowly and prayerfully. Ask God to inject hunger into your spirit—to give you an ever-increasing hunger for Him.

> One thing I ask of the LORD, this is what I seek: that I may dwell in the house of the LORD all the days of my life, to gaze upon the beauty of the LORD and to seek him in his temple. (Ps. 27:4)

> You will seek me and find me when you seek me with all your heart. (Jer. 29:13)

> Blessed are those who hunger and thirst for righteousness, for they will be filled. (Matt. 5:6)

> If anyone is thirsty, let him come to me and drink. Whoever believes in me, as the Scripture has said, streams of living water will flow from within him. (John 7:37–38)

> O God, you are my God, earnestly I seek you; my soul thirsts for you, my body longs for you, in a dry and weary land where there is no water. (Ps. 63:1)

> As the deer pants for streams of water, so my soul pants for you, O God. My soul thirsts for God, for the living God. Where can I go and meet with God? (Ps. 42:1–2)

Come, all you who are thirsty, come to the waters; and you who have no money, come, buy and eat! Come, buy wine and milk without money and without cost. (Isa. 55:1)

Lord Jesus, what You are teaching me today is _____

_____

Lord Jesus, the action step that I will take is _____

_____

Day 3

REPENT

When Jesus announced the coming of His kingdom, He told His disciples how to get ready for it. It was simple and straightforward, a single word: "repent"! "Repent, for the kingdom of heaven is near" (Matt. 4:17), Jesus told them. John, the baptizer, whose entire ministry was designed to get people ready for the rapid advancement of Christ's kingdom, announced identical words (see 3:2). Repentance is always on the front end of every move of God. The Bible calls repentance a gift (see Acts 5:31; 11:18; 2 Tim. 2:25), and as with every gift He gives, God wants us to open this gift and put it to good use. For this reason, as Christ introduces you to *church on fire*, He will certainly activate repentance in your life and experience.

The Greek word translated "repent" is *metanoeo*, which means a complete change of mind, perspective, disposition, orientation and motivation.[1] To repent is to have a revolutionary change of mind that brings about a revolutionary change of heart that brings about a revolutionary change of conduct that brings about a revolutionary change of lifestyle.

What Is God Doing?

As Christ began to teach me to repent and as my appetite to spend extended time in His presence began to grow, I invited my mentor Armin Gesswein to facilitate a prayer weekend in my church in South Florida. My church loved Armin and responded well to his practical teaching. The highlight of that week came for me during a private lunch with this man of God. Over another large bowl of lettuce—Armin loved salad— he smiled and asked me a most probing and unsettling question: "Fred, you've told me a lot about what you're doing at your church, but may I ask you, what is *God* doing at your church?" That question knocked the wind right out of me. It was very much a fair question—a kingdom question— but one that ran completely contrary to my thought process. I was a well-trained seminary graduate with degrees from Wheaton College and Gordon-Conwell Theological Seminary. I had been taught what I was to do at church, and my congregation was effectively growing as a result. I was so preoccupied with what I was doing at church that I never gave a thought to what Christ was doing.

I paused, stammered, hemmed and hawed. I fumbled for answers. After five or six false starts, I bit my lip and humbled myself. "Mr. Gesswein, I hate to admit it," I explained, "but I am not sure what God is doing in my church. I could talk for hours about what I am doing, but I cannot put my finger on one thing that God is doing in my church." It was pitiful but true.

That question—what is God doing in your church?—was my call to repentance, my call to change my thinking, my perspective, my disposition, my orientation and my motivation. In many ways it introduced me to a whole new world of *church on fire*. It shifted my focus away from me, my work and my self-efforts and onto God's work. It pointed me to start welcoming God into the church and to focus on what He was doing.

Over the next seventeen years, Armin Gesswein would frequently call me and challenge me, "So Fred, tell me about what Christ is doing in your church these days." I must admit that there were times when I didn't have much to share, but normally I had some significant stories about God's activity. From that first day on, however, no matter how many times he asked me that question, I never minded. In fact, I got to a point where I was the one who would call Armin to say, "Wait until you hear about what God is doing in our church these days!"

Now let me ask you a personal question: in your church, what is more important to you—what you do or what God does? Think about it. This is no trivial question. In your church, what do you think about more—what you do or what God does? What do you more eagerly anticipate each week—what you do or what God does? What do you spend more time planning for—what you do or what God does? These questions are worth taking the rest of the day off just to think about. They may even lead you to repentance just as they led me.

Learning to Pray

None of us knows how to pray as we ought. In one way or another, we all learn to pray in the same way—as an act of repentance. Even the early disciples learned to pray as an act of repentance. Jesus invited them to His favorite prayer garden at the base of the Mount of Olives known as Gethsemane. Here they were with the Lord on the final night of His life, and they couldn't even keep their eyes open. Even after Jesus had given them three years of round-the-clock mentoring, training and equipping, providing them with front-row seats to witness His spectacular miracles and a backstage pass to listen to Him debrief at the end of every day, these men still did not have a clue as to how to pray. Three times in the prayer garden that night Jesus urged them to pray with him, and three times they fell fast asleep. It was as if they kept hitting the snooze alarm. Jesus kept waking by asking them the familiar question, "Could you not pray with Me one hour?" and three times they dozed off (see Matt. 26:36–45).

But then something happened. A few weeks later this same band of wimpy, prayerless disciples were radically changed. They went from being eleven men who couldn't keep their eyes open to a group of one hundred twenty upper-room disciples who wouldn't be denied. They went from not even being able to pray for one measly hour into a band of warriors who could pray ten straight days—two hundred forty hours!

The critical element in this story is that the disciples' shocking prayerlessness was preceded by their pride. Nothing kills prayerful desperation faster than pride and self-sufficiency. When Peter had announced a few hours earlier at the final Passover meal, "All others may deny You, Lord, but not me" (see Mark 14:29), he was obviously in serious trouble. When he pompously proceeded to claim, "I am ready to go to prison or even to die for You" (see Luke 22:33), it was just a matter of hours before he would stumble and fall. He may have swaggered into the garden of prayer in Gethsemane that eventful night, but he would come crawling out with his tail between his legs like a whipped puppy. He would be humbled, broken and keenly aware of his own personal inadequacies. Within six hours of their gathering in the garden, he would deny Christ three times. But the real story is that prideful Peter was led to repentance, and out of his repentance he became prayerful Peter.

So what changed in the disciples to create the praying people who would build a praying church? Simple: they repented. They repented of prideful prayerlessness. They repented of an over-inflated view of their own self-importance and a shrunken view of Christ. The kingdom of God was about to overtake them in the upper room on Pentecost, and Jesus was getting them ready by leading them to repentance.

If you have ever looked at your church and thought, *we will never become a praying church*, or even more personally, if you have looked in the mirror and said, *I will never become a praying person*, I want to encourage you. Just think about the low octane prayer life of the disciples before Pentecost. Since the disciples dozed off during their final night of prayer with Jesus, take heart—there is certainly hope for the rest of us. Just wait until you see what Christ can do with your church family. He knows how to build praying people and praying churches, that's for sure.

Since none of us knows how to pray as we ought, in one way or another we all learn to pray the same way—as an act of repentance. Peter reminds me of how I stormed into church ministry with a swagger, thinking that I could knock 'em dead. Little did I know that I would almost kill myself with misguided zeal and a root of arrogance, pride and self-sufficiency a mile long. Pride and prayerlessness are a fatal cocktail.

Now It's Your Turn: Day 3 Action Step

Repent of your prayerlessness. Repentance always begins with new obedience to Christ. Repenting of prayerlessness brings heaven and earth together in a hurry. Now is a good time for you to repent of pride and prayerlessness. Remember, repentance is a complete change of mind, perspective, disposition, orientation and motivation. Throughout our thirty-one-day adventure, we will learn that in the kingdom of God, repentance is an ongoing activity and that there is no better time to repent than now.

Today I repent specifically of _____

_____

Lord Jesus, what You are teaching me today is _____

_____

Lord Jesus, the action step that I will take is _____

_____

Day 4

RECEIVE

The advancing of Christ's kingdom rises and falls on our ability to receive from Him. The fact is, we have nothing to give that we didn't first receive. "Freely you have received, freely give," Jesus said (Matt. 10:8). As you get ready to encounter the manifest presence of Christ in your personal life as well as with your church family, God wants to activate your receptors.

When the College of Prayer was first invited to Jordan in the Middle East, we were told by local church leaders how desperate the church in that country was. One of the dear leaders we spoke to had seen a vision of God using the College of Prayer to serve as a catalyst for igniting fire in the church. Nine different congregations from various parts of Jordan met together with us for three days of worship-based, God-encountering prayer. During the opening session I encouraged the group of ninety-five believers to hold their hands out toward the Lord and to repeat a simple but dangerous prayer:

> Father, I receive right now the infilling of the Holy Spirit in the name of the Lord Jesus Christ. Open my spiritual eyes that I may see and recognize what You are doing. Open my spiritual ears that I might hear what You are saying. Come heal and activate my receptors that I might receive from You in these days all that You have for me.

I explained from the Bible that when Christ manifests His presence to us, He will activate our sensory perception. When Isaiah had his magnificent encounter with God, many levels of sensory perception were activated:

- God activated his sight: "I saw the Lord . . . high and lifted up" (Isa. 6:1, NKJV).

- God activated his hearing: "They were calling . . . 'Holy, holy, holy is the LORD Almighty; the whole earth is full of his glory'" (6:3).

- God activated his sense of touch: "The doorposts and thresholds shook" (6:4).

- God activated his sense of smell: "And the temple was filled with smoke" (6:4).

Throughout the Bible we see examples of God figuratively activating the senses:

Taste and see that the LORD is good. (Ps. 34:8)

Open my eyes that I may see wonderful things in your law. (119:18)

Blessed are the pure in heart, for they will see God. (Matt. 5:8)

I pray also that the eyes of your hearts may be enlightened. (Eph. 1:18)

The following story may stretch your theological envelope, but I was worshiping Christ one Sunday in my church in Atlanta, and I smelled the most beautiful fragrance. I sniffed the person to my right, and it was not her. I sniffed the person to my left, whose hands were raised in worship, and it was definitely not him. I asked one of our intercessors standing near me, "Do you smell that?"

"Yes," he answered. "That's the healing presence of Christ. He is here to heal today."

After the next song was finished, I grabbed a microphone and invited people with sickness and physical infirmities to come to the front for healing prayer. That morning many people came, and a dozen or more people received healing.

I can't explain why God chose to activate our ability to smell His presence on that particular morning, but He did. I share this story not to sound sensational and certainly not to distract us with manifestations but rather to illustrate the wide range of means by which we can receive from God. At the College of Prayer, we teach our people never to seek manifestations—not even to seek an experience. Rather, we teach them to seek an encounter with Christ and to leave the manifestations to Him. God knows how to appropriately manifest Himself at the proper time; we just want our receivers to be ready to respond appropriately.

More Receiving Meetings

In some ways we don't need more prayer meetings; we need more receiving meetings. When we put the emphasis on prayer, we can unintentionally take the emphasis off what God does and put it back on what we do: we pray. However, when we shift the focus off of what we do and put the focus back on what God does, we will proportionately spend more time receiving while we are praying.

As a young pastor, God opened my eyes to this principle soon after He delivered me from prayerlessness. Almost every time I would pray, I sensed the Holy Spirit telling me, "Hold out your hands." I would obediently extend empty hands, palms up to Christ as I would pray. It served as a powerful, demonstrative reminder to me that God wants me not only to pray but to receive.

Have you ever recognized that the entire Lord's prayer pattern (see Matt. 6:9–13) is all about receiving?

"Our Father"—God became our Father when we received new life in Christ.

"Hallowed be your name"—we receive the revelation of the virtue of His name.

"Your kingdom come"—we receive His advancing kingdom.

"Your will be done"—we receive the accomplishment of His will.

"Give us today our daily bread"—we receive God's provision for physical needs.

"Forgive us"—we receive God's provision for spiritual needs.

"As we also have forgiven our debtors"—we give what we first received.

"Lead us"—we receive God's leadership.

"Deliver us"—we receive God's deliverance.

At the end of the Lord's prayer pattern, we appropriately give everything back to Him: "Yours is the kingdom and the power and the glory forever" (Matt. 6:13, NASB).

No, It's Not Selfish

People have challenged me on this emphasis of receiving, suggesting, "Isn't it selfish to always be receiving?" No. It is not a matter of selfishness, it's a matter of dependence. Just look at the example of Christ Himself—He was always receiving, because He lived in a constant state of dependence on the Father:

> The Son . . . can do only what he sees his Father doing. (John 5:19)

> By myself I can do nothing. (5:30)

> I have come down from heaven not to do my will but to do the will of him who sent me. (6:38)

> No one can come to me unless the Father who sent me draws him. (6:44)

> My teaching is not my own. It comes from him who sent me. (7:16)

> The one who sent me is with me; he has not left me alone, for I always do what pleases him. (8:29)

> I did not speak of my own accord, but the Father who sent me commanded me what to say and how to say it. (12:49)

> As the Father has loved me, so have I loved you. (15:9)

> If you obey my commands, you will remain in my love, just as I have obeyed my Father's commands and remain in his love. (15:10)

> I have brought you glory on earth by completing the work you gave me to do. (17:4)

> Now they know that everything you have given me comes from you. (17:7)

> I gave them the words you gave me and they accepted them. They knew with certainty that I came from you, and they believed that you sent me. (17:8)

Because Jesus lived in complete dependence on His Father in a constant state of receiving, it should not surprise us to realize how frequently He exhorted His disciples to remain in an active state of receiving:

> I say to you: Ask and it will be given to you; seek and you will find; knock and the door will be opened to you. (Luke 11:9)

> Everyone who asks receives; he who seeks finds; and to him who knocks, the door will be opened. (11:10)

I tell you, whatever you ask for in prayer, believe that you have received it, and it will be yours. (Mark 11:24)

A man can receive nothing unless it has been given him from heaven. (John 3:27, NASB)

Until now you have not asked for anything in my name. Ask and you will receive, and your joy will be complete. (16:24)

Receive the Holy Spirit. (20:22)

You will receive power when the Holy Spirit comes on you; and you will be my witnesses in Jerusalem, and in all Judea and Samaria, and to the ends of the earth. (Acts 1:8)

Armin Gesswein frequently said, "There is a difference between praying for revival and revival praying. When you simply pray for revival, you can pray yourself into unbelief, praying revival further and further off into the future. But when you engage in revival-prayer, you receive right now a portion of that toward which you are praying." Notice that the difference between these two types of prayer is receiving. If "praying for revival" describes your prayer life in the past, I encourage you to step out of simply praying for some future revival and to begin receiving right now a portion of that which God wants to more fully give you and your church family.

Now It's Your Turn: Day 4 Action Step

Carefully reread the verses in day four. Observe closely how receiving-conscious Jesus was. Consider how receiving-conscious He helped His disciples become. Ask Christ to make you and your church family more receiving-conscious. In a sense, the entire discipleship ministry of Jesus was to prepare His followers to receive in the upper room the mother lode of all downloads: the fullness and baptism of the Holy Spirit. In the weeks to come, you will learn what it means to corporately receive the outpouring and infilling of the Holy Spirit in your local church. Today, however, you have an opportunity to receive personally. The prayer that the Jordanian believers prayed is a good place to start:

Father, I receive right now the infilling of the Holy Spirit in the name of the Lord Jesus Christ. Open my eyes that I may see and recognize what You are doing. Open my ears that I might hear what You are saying.

Come heal and activate my receptors that I might receive from You in these days all that You have for me.

Lord Jesus, what You are teaching me today is _____

_____

Lord Jesus, the action step that I will take is _____

_____

Day 5

OPEN YOUR EYES

Stories of the handiwork of Christ are powerful. When we allow the people in our sphere of ministry to use their own words to describe their encounters with Christ, it is as if we are taking the lid off what God is doing among us. The result is infectious.

Susana had worn Coke-bottle-thick eyeglasses since she was nine years old. As an employee in a fabric store, when her eyeglasses broke, it created a major challenge—how could she read the tiny print on the clothing patterns to help her customers?

That evening her eight-year-old daughter Tammy announced, "It will be OK, Mommy. I have prayed for you."

"Yes, Tammy," Susana said. "God will provide money for us to get my glasses fixed."

"Oh no, Mommy. I have asked God to heal your eyes so that you can read the fine print."

Susana wept at her own unbelief in contrast to her daughter's high level of faith. The next morning Susana woke up and realized that she could see perfectly. Her eyes had been miraculously healed. When she told her story to our church family, she wept again for joy at the startling faith her daughter had displayed in God's ability in contrast to her own unbelief. This story, as you can imagine, was catalytic to inspire the faith of many other people in our congregation to believe God for healing on that Sunday.

The Power of Stories in the Gospels

Many times throughout the Gospels we see how Jesus leveraged people's stories to advance His kingdom and raise people's faith levels.

When Jesus sat and interacted with the Samaritan woman, she felt loved and accepted. Christ restored her dignity. It is no wonder that the Gospel of John includes the summary statement, "Many of the Samaritans from that town believed in him because of the woman's testimony, 'He told me everything I ever did'" (John 4:39). Because of the woman's testimony, when the Samaritans came to Jesus, they urged Him to stay with them, and He stayed two days. "And because of his words many more became believers" (John 4:41).

The demonized man who lived on the banks of the Sea of Galilee in the region of the Gerasenes became the subject of one of the most dramatic, life-transforming stories in the Gospels. He lived in the cemetery and had such supernatural strength that he could break iron chains with his bare hands. No one could subdue him. He was tormented day and night and often cut himself with stones. He felt tortured, rejected and alone. When Christ freed him from his demons, he was a changed man. Jesus told him to return to his hometown and tell his story: "Go home to your family and tell them how much the Lord has done for you, and how he has had mercy on you" (Mark 5:19).

The next time Jesus returned to this same area, it is not surprising to find that the crowds were larger than ever: "As soon as they got out of the boat, people recognized Jesus. They ran throughout that whole region and carried the sick on mats to wherever they heard he was" (Mark 6:54–55). The vigorous response from the crowds was due to the power of one man's testimony.

A God Journal

Years ago I was convinced that journals were for girls or sissies. A real man would never use a journal, or so I thought. I was eating breakfast with Henry Blackaby at Cracker Barrel early one morning. He and I both lived in Atlanta, so I had met with this godly man to ask a few questions, and I listened to him offer one kingdom principle after another.

When he learned I did not journal, he looked puzzled. "If you spot a twenty dollar bill on the sidewalk," he asked, "would you bend over and pick it up?"

"Sure. I still pick up pennies," I admitted.

"Do you have a place to put your twenty dollar bills?"

Again, I nodded. "Sure."

He leaned across his bowl of oatmeal, looked straight into my soul and asked me with a half smile, "What's worth more—a word from God or a twenty dollar bill?" He knew he had me. "Fred, when you hear God's word and when you see God at work, you want to have a place to write it down."

He proceeded to explain, "A journal is not your story; a journal is God's story. It's where we record the activity of God. The more we record, the more effectively we learn to hear His voice and recognize His activity around us."

That breakfast with Henry Blackaby took place eighteen years ago. On the shelves in my study, I now have twenty-one God journals filled with the words and works of God. Journaling has become one of the most life-giving disciplines for me.

The pastoral team at my church decided that they too wanted to start a God journal. Every week as we meet for our team meeting, we pull out our God journal, share stories of God's activity among us and record the activity of God in our church family life. We also have started what we affectionately call a Book of Life in which we record the names of every single person who prays to receive Christ as a result of our church ministries. Even the elder team in our church has now started its own God journal.

A God journal is beneficial on many levels:

- It puts the spotlight on God and His activities. A God journal is a wonderful way to shift our focus to what God is doing in our church and away from what we are doing.

- It helps us learn to hear God's voice. Some people call this prophetic journaling—to write down what you hear the Holy Spirit saying to you while you are praying.

- It helps us learn how to recognize what God is doing around us. Jesus said, "The Son can do nothing by himself; he can do only what he sees his Father doing" (John 5:19). Just as Jesus recognized His Father's work around Him, we want to learn how to recognize the Father's activity as well.

Remember, the God journal is not our story; it's God's story. We don't want to use it to record our own activity but God's activity. Our pastoral team writes only two things in our God journal: God's work, and God's words.

Now It's Your Turn: Day 5 Action Step

Consider starting your own personal God journal in which you can write the works and words of God—where you see Him working and what you hear Him saying. In cooperation with your lead pastor, you may also want to start a congregation-wide God journal for your church family.

Lord Jesus, what You are teaching me today is _____

_____

Lord Jesus, the action step that I will take is _____

_____

Week 1: Questions for Small Groups

1. Have someone in your group read aloud Luke 11:1–13.
2. What do you learn from these verses about prayer?
3. When Fred thought he was dying of extreme chest pain, what did God teach him? Can you relate? Tell your story.
4. Why is prayerlessness such an indicator of pride and self-reliance?
5. What has God used in your life to bring you to the place of repentance from prayerlessness?
6. Why is the short, five-word prayer "Lord, teach us to pray" such a strategic prayer? Be specific.
7. As a guest walks into your church, what does he or she think is more important to you—what you and your people do at church or what God does?
8. Right now where do you see God at work in your church?
9. If the Holy Spirit were to leave your church (this is purely hypothetical), which activities would end and which activities would continue pretty much as they are?
10. Dream a little. Over the next thirty-one days, when God begins to more consistently manifest His presence in your church, what might it look like? Be specific.

Week 1: Advice for Pastors

Throughout the following weeks of our adventure, you will want to prayerfully consider which God-encountering, life-transforming stories of the people in your church will be most effective for you to share publicly. Stories are faith building and infectious. If you choose to take your church through this thirty-one-day adventure corporately, it will be helpful to pray publicly for the adventure during Sunday worship.

Some of us may swagger into ministry, but we will never swagger into the upper room. If you are not aware of your own personal inadequacies or if you think somehow that you have it in yourself to serve your people in your own strength, then even though I haven't met you, I can tell you something about yourself: you are exhausted. You may even be on the verge of burnout. Please do yourself a favor: repent. Quit the game. Get off the church treadmill. Repent of an over-inflated view of your own self-importance. Repent of your self-sufficient swagger. Repent of your prayerlessness.

This thirty-one-day adventure is designed to lead local churches to encounter the manifest presence of Christ. While it will certainly be beneficial for you personally, you will receive the fullest impact by taking this journey together with a small group of other Christ followers, with your leadership team or with your entire church family. You must decide what is best in your particular setting at this specific time. This next week in particular is all about building your core prayer group and bringing them along with you. This is what Jesus did when He built praying disciples.

Week Two

GATHER FOR FIRE

The first miracle of the ascended Christ was gathering His disciples into the upper room. The second miracle was pouring out His Holy Spirit into the upper-room gathering on the Day of Pentecost. The third miracle of the ascended Christ was to win three thousand Jews to faith in Christ in one hour.

Our Baptist brothers and sisters celebrate the third miracle. Our Pentecostal brothers and sisters celebrate the second miracle. But we all need to realize that without the first miracle, there would be no second or third miracle. It's easy to overlook the first miracle—gathering together the 120 upper-room disciples into the God-encountering prayer meeting. This first miracle in the early church is the first miracle God wants to perform in your church, and it is our focus in week two of our adventure.

Building a God-encountering, praying church will require every ounce of leadership muscle you have. It did for Jesus. Just think; when Christ ascended to heaven, all He left behind on earth was a prayer meeting. The three years of Jesus' systematic discipleship resulted in gathering 120 believers in the upper room for a God-encountering prayer meeting. Make no mistake about it—this upper-room gathering was the first miracle of the ascended Christ. He gathered His followers into the upper room so that He might pour His Holy Spirit into them and then thrust them forth as empowered workers from that upper room to advance His kingdom and fulfill His mission throughout the world. Building the upper room is the first step in the strategic plan of Christ's method. Without this pre-Pentecost prayer gathering, there would not have been Pentecost power, and there certainly would never have been post-Pentecost discipling of all nations.

Week two of our thirty-one-day adventure is where you will begin to link arms with other praying friends. You will begin to gather God's people for worship-based, God-encountering prayer in an upper-room environment. Before you run off to reach the nations or even to love your neighbors, you will begin to gather and build an environment to welcome the manifest presence of Christ.

Day 6

COME UNDER ORDERS

You could probably build a deck by yourself in your backyard if you tried. You might even be able to add a room onto your house if you put your mind to it. To build an upper-room, God-encountering prayer gathering for your church family, however, will require teamwork.

Jim Cymbala, pastor of the Brooklyn Tabernacle, knows from experience that building an upper room is not for wimps. When he arrived as lead pastor of the Brooklyn Tabernacle, there were only a handful of people in attendance. In his own words, things were so bad at his run-down church that his family didn't want to attend. He admits that at times the worship services were so bad that even he didn't want to show up! Then one day Cymbala sensed God forcefully speaking to him deep down in his soul.

"If you and your wife will lead my people to pray and call upon my name, you will never lack for something fresh to preach. I will supply all the money that's needed, both for the church and for your family, and you will never have a building large enough to contain the crowds I will send in response."[1]

He was overwhelmed by these hopeful words. He wept. He knew that he had heard from God. "From this day on," Cymbala told his congregation, "the prayer meeting will be the barometer of our church. What happens on Tuesday night will be the gauge by which we will judge success or failure because that will be the measure by which God blesses us."[2]

Within a couple of weeks the Brooklyn Tabernacle began to see dramatic answers to specific prayers. New people started coming each week. Word spread throughout Brooklyn that God was at the tabernacle, and if a person had deep needs, that was the place for him or her. Drug addicts, prostitutes, homeless people, pimps and transvestites started to come to church. The power of the gospel was released into the daily lives of needy people, and it all happened in response to prayer.

Today thousands of people from all over New York City and beyond gather not only to worship on Sundays at the Brooklyn Tabernacle but also to pray together every Tuesday night. They experience firsthand the reality of reaching a hurting world through a revived church. The reformation of the Brooklyn Tabernacle did not start in a committee meeting; it started in a prayer meeting. The impact of this church in the New York City area and around the world today comes from an upper-room, God-encountering prayer meeting. Jim Cymbala and the Brooklyn Tabernacle are following the same method that Jesus implemented two thousand years ago.

Do Not Leave Jerusalem

When Jesus built His upper-room disciples, it was no easy task. The night Jesus was betrayed, His disciples were not yet upper-room disciples. Not even close! When He took the Twelve to the prayer garden in Gethsemane, three times He pleaded with them to pray, and three times they dozed off. They couldn't even keep their eyes open for one single hour. So what did Jesus do to get these disciples into the upper room? He put them under strict orders:

> On one occasion, while he was eating with them, he gave them this command: "Do not leave Jerusalem, but wait for the gift my Father promised, which you have heard me speak about. For John baptized with water, but in a few days you will be baptized with the Holy Spirit." (Acts 1:4–5)

The word for "command" is the Greek word *paraggello*,[3] the strongest word for command in the Greek language. It means "to put under military orders, to charge or mandate." When Jesus sent His disciples back to the upper room, He did not give them a take-it-or-leave-it suggestion; this was a command! They obeyed with immediate action: "They went upstairs to the room where they were staying" (Acts 1:13).

Don't underestimate the weight of this mandate. It sat over the disciples like a drawn sword or a flashing neon light. "Do not leave Jerusalem" was one of the classic seek-first-the-kingdom-of-God-and-all-other-things-will-be-added-to-you moments. It established prayer as the disciples' first work. Before we plan, preach, promote, make disciples or reach nations, we pray. We pray, and we receive. We receive power in the fullness of Christ so that we can then effectively fulfill all our other assignments.

"Do not leave Jerusalem" establishes our first assignment as ministering to the presence of the Lord. All other assignments are secondary.

The final command Jesus gave should not be taken lightly. "Do not leave Jerusalem" was as much of a command as "do not commit adultery" or "do not murder." These four words moved the disciples into the upper room. Archimedes said, "Give me a lever big enough and a fulcrum on which to place it, and I will move the world." This final command of Christ was the disciples' lever. The fulcrum was the sovereign authority of Almighty God. With this single command Jesus moved His disciples from returning to their fishing nets in Galilee to move forward into the unchartered waters of the upper room.

Now It's Your Turn: Day 6 Action Step

Today it is time to begin building your upper room. In the days to come, you will take steps to bring others along with you, but today it starts with you. My mentor Armin Gesswein frequently said, "If you want to get revival, draw a circle around yourself and pray, 'Lord, revive everyone within this circle!'" Take time right now to pray this dangerous prayer.

What does "do not leave Jerusalem" mean to you personally? What changes need to be made in your life and in your schedule for you to come under orders the way the disciples did? Be specific.

Lord Jesus, what You are teaching me today is _____

_____

Lord Jesus, the action step that I will take is _____

_____

Day 7

MINISTER TO THE PRESENCE OF THE LORD

Today we are introduced to a life-giving principle that may be new to you—the high calling of ministry to the presence of the Lord. It doesn't matter if you are a business owner, a school teacher, a sales person, a computer programmer or an airline pilot; if you intend to be an upper-room disciple, your first assignment is to minister to the presence of the Lord. This is your first responsibility as you face any new day. Every other responsibility comes second. When Paul, Barnabas and a band of praying prophets gathered in the upper room in Antioch, they gathered for one solitary purpose: to minister to the presence of the Lord—"As they ministered to the Lord and fasted, the Holy Spirit said, 'Now separate to Me Barnabas and Saul for the work to which I have called them'" (Acts 13:2, NKJV).

We are well-familiar with the phrase *ministry for the Lord* or even *ministering to the Lord*, but we who recognize the manifest presence of the Lord are invited to respond to His manifest presence as the highest treasure in life. When we recognize that we were made for His manifest presence, we have no problem lingering in His presence and enjoying every minute of it. "One thing I ask of the LORD, this is what I seek: that I may dwell in the house of the LORD all the days of my life, to gaze upon the beauty of the LORD and to seek him in his temple" (Ps. 27:4). The concept of ministering to the Lord may be foreign to your experience, but it was not foreign to Jewish worshipers. In many places in the Old Testament, we see that priests were assigned to do nothing but to minister to the presence of the Lord. David appointed Levitical priests to minister to the Lord (see 1 Chron. 15:2). The sons of Zadok were the Levites who were assigned to minister before the Lord (see Ezek. 40:46; Joel 1:9, 13; 2:17). Samuel learned as a youth to minister before the Lord (see 1 Sam. 2:11). In Christ we are all priests (see 1 Pet. 2:5, 9) who are given the same access to come boldly before the throne of grace and to minister to Him (see Heb. 4:16).

A Matter of Worship

Ministering to the Lord is a make-it-or-break-it issue. You will never become an upper-room disciple, and you will never build a praying church until you learn to minister to the presence of Christ. If you genuinely intend to welcome the manifest presence of Christ as a church family, it only makes sense that you need to first learn what it means to minister to His presence. When you value the manifest presence of Christ enough to linger in God's presence and gaze upon His beauty, then God will entrust you with more of His manifest presence. If you do not value the presence of Christ enough to stand in His presence and minister to His presence, why would He choose to continue to manifest Himself to you? After all, Jesus said, "Do not give dogs what is sacred; do not throw your pearls to pigs" (Matt. 7:6). There is no greater pearl than the pearl of Christ's manifest presence.

Too many Christians view prayer as religious rather than relational. For this reason, they see prayer as something they do rather than as who they are—something to check off their to-do list rather than a life-sustaining necessity. Such people can treat the fire of God's manifest presence with the same cavalier attitude. When will we learn that if Christ lives to pray (see Heb. 7:25), then we too would do well to live to pray—and embrace a prayer lifestyle? Since Christ is the manifest presence of God, and one day the dwelling of God will be with us forever (see Rev. 21:3), we want to get used to dwelling in His manifest presence now and to cultivating an ongoing prayer lifestyle. We are eternally called to pray and eternally called to the fire.

It is a kingdom principle that in the very act of being worshiped, God often chooses to reveal Himself. As we minister to, or worship, the presence of Christ, He will often reveal more of Himself to us.

Our First Assignment

Our first assignment is to minister to the presence of God. It is only logical that Christ will not entrust us with assignments two, three, four or five until we fulfill assignment number one.

When I arrived in Atlanta to pastor Lilburn Alliance Church in 1988, I was overwhelmed by my new job. Within the first few days, the Holy Spirit made it very clear to me, "The primary reason I have called you here to Atlanta is to worship Me." That set me straight.

I travel several times a year with the College of Prayer to countries all over the world. Whenever I arrive in another country, the Holy Spirit always reminds me, "The reason I called you here is primarily to worship Me. Before you do anything else, I want you to fulfill your first assignment. Worship Me first, and then I will give you your second assignment."

No one was more keenly aware of his assignment to take the gospel to all the nations than the apostle Paul, yet with that on his shoulders, he also knew the greater weight of his first assignment: to minister to the presence of the Lord. Once he fulfilled his primary assignment, then he received from the Holy Spirit his secondary assignment: "Set apart for me Barnabas and Saul for the work to which I have called them" (Acts 13:2).

I am frequently asked, "What sets apart an upper-room prayer meeting from any other prayer meeting?" Easy. Most prayer meetings have an agenda—pray for church ministries, missionaries, children and such. When we gather in the upper room, however, we have only one item on our agenda—to minister to the presence of the Lord.

Now It's Your Turn: Day 7 Action Step

The best way to learn to minister to the presence of Christ is to minister to the presence of Christ. Spend a full hour—a solid sixty minutes—today or tomorrow alone with Him. No social media. No music. No phone. No distractions. Just sit at Jesus' feet, and enjoy His presence. Treat yourself to the best hour you will have spent in a long time. Block off your schedule so that you can spend an uninterrupted extended time with God.

As David did, ask God to give you an undivided heart: "Teach me your way, O LORD, and I will walk in your truth; give me an undivided heart, that I may fear your name" (Ps. 86:11). Ask Him to make you a person of *one thing*:

> *One thing* I ask of the LORD, this is what I seek: that I may dwell in the house of the LORD all the days of my life, to gaze upon the beauty of the LORD and to seek him in his temple. (27:4)

> "Martha, Martha," the Lord answered, "you are worried and upset about many things, but only *one thing* is needed. Mary has chosen what is better, and it will not be taken away from her." (Luke 10:41–42)

> Brothers, I do not consider myself yet to have taken hold of it. But *one thing* I do: Forgetting what is behind and straining toward what is ahead, I press on toward the goal to win the prize for which God has called me heavenward in Christ Jesus. (Phil. 3:13–14)

Lord Jesus, what You are teaching me today is _____

_____

Lord Jesus, the action step that I will take is _____

_____

Day 8

CLEAR YOUR CALENDAR

For some of us it's probably the sports bar, Starbucks or our man cave. In the Middle East, however, when it was time to hang out with friends, people went to the upper room—a quiet, secluded place to think, talk, clear their head, sip a beverage, tell some stories and unwind at the end of a long day. It was this common place that Jesus selected to become the centerpiece of civilization.

The upper room is the crown jewel of Jesus' discipleship ministry. It is also the closest we can get to heaven on earth. The membrane that separates heaven and earth thins out in the upper room. God draws near to His people as His people draw near to Him. It is in this room that Christ chooses to manifest His presence in conspicuous, unmistakable ways. He speaks. He works. Most importantly, He shows His face in the upper room.

The upper room, or *huperoon* in Greek,[1] is common throughout the Middle East. The square-shaped Mediterranean buildings provide ideal flat, open space on the rooftops where people gather for conversation—to sip tea, tell their stories, welcome out-of-town guests and unwind at the end of the day. For Jesus and His disciples, it offered an ideal meeting place where they could talk, pray, plan and eat together. When Jesus told His followers, "Do not leave Jerusalem" (Acts 1:4), they knew immediately where to go: "They went upstairs to the room [*huperoon*]" (Acts 1:13).

Bible scholar F.F. Bruce says, "In Jerusalem the apostles went to the place where their company was lodging in Jerusalem—the upper chamber. It is possible . . . that this is the room where Jesus and His disciples had kept the Passover on the eve of His execution . . . may also have been the room where He appeared to some of them in Jerusalem after He rose from the dead."[2] The great Bible commentator R.C.H. Lenski described the *huperoon* as a place for retirement and quiet and, for the company here described, a place that was free from interruption and disturbance.[3]

The tragedy of the modern church is that the crown jewel of Jesus' discipleship ministry has largely become the flagrant omission. We need to learn again how to rebuild the upper room.

The Five Upper-Room Features

Every room has five basic elements: a door, an atmosphere, walls, floor and ceiling. These same five elements are useful to describe the five features of the upper room. These are critical for us to understand if we are going to rebuild the upper room.

1. The door to the upper room is low—it's the doorway of humility and obedience. The disciples entered the upper room conscious of their own weakness. They came low before the Lord in obedience to His command, "Do not leave Jerusalem."

2. The atmosphere in the upper room is unity. It says of the upper-room disciples, "They all joined together constantly in prayer" (Acts 1:14). And ten days after they first gathered, it says, "When the day of Pentecost came, they were all together in one place" (Acts 2:1). It was most remarkable for 120 people to be in the same room, nonstop for ten days, in perfect unity. Why such unity? Simple. The single focus in the upper room is Christ, and when we encounter Christ, we no longer have any hidden agendas, no selfish ambition, no bitter jealousies, no elbowing for position or climbing over others to demand attention. The unity in the room is based on the fact that when we encounter the manifest presence of Christ, we have one purpose, one faith, one hope, one baptism and one Lord. We have unity.

3. The walls around the upper room are walls of separation that keep out distractions. Many upper rooms in the Middle East have stem walls that are waist high (not full load-bearing walls) to keep people from falling off and also to afford a degree of privacy. These stone walls represent parameters of separation. Similarly, the early disciples—all 120 of them—canceled every other appointment they had on their calendar in order to make time to meet with Christ in uninterrupted, extended prayer and worship. For you and me to become upper-room disciples, we too need to erect walls of separation to keep out distractions from other commitments on our calendars. Let's face it. Many of us church

leaders are pulled in too many directions. Even Bill Hybels—who certainly knows a busy schedule—says that he is "too busy not to pray."[4] Upper-room disciples do not give God their leftovers and spare time; upper-room disciples give God whatever time He wants. He deserves our best time. Since I am a morning person, I meet with God in the morning because I want my time with Him to be robust, alert and responsive. When I schedule time for our church to pray, I don't look for the leftovers in our church calendar. Instead I pick the best time of each week in which to schedule our prayer times.

4. The floorboards in the upper room rattle with anticipation. The early disciples were expectant when they gathered in the upper room because Christ had given them the promise of the Father (see Acts 1:4). Jesus had told them that He would clothe them with power (see Luke 24:49), and they believed it. They were overwhelmed by both the enormity of the assignment and the reality that Christ was now back in heaven. You can easily imagine how their desperation quickly became anticipation and expectation.

5. The ceiling in the upper room is wide open. Most upper rooms in the Middle East have no roof. Some have cloth to shield them from the sun, but essentially they have an open ceiling. This is a picture of an open heaven. It was into this first upper room in Jerusalem that God poured out His Holy Spirit. "All of them were filled with the Holy Spirit and began to speak in other tongues as the Spirit enabled them" (Acts 2:4).

For this reason we can say that the upper room was the crown jewel of Jesus' discipleship ministry. Gathering 120 young Jewish-background believers in Jerusalem for ten days of worship-based, God-encountering prayer immediately following His ascension into heaven was no small feat. It was something that He had systematically built for three years. The upper room today is conspicuously missing from too many of our churches. How can the crown jewel of the early church be the flagrant omission in any church? Something needs to change.

The most difficult part of building a praying church could well be deciding when to schedule your upper-room, God-encountering prayer meeting. In order for you to build a praying church, you will need to take dominion over your church calendar.

This reminds me of the story that my friend and fellow prayer mobilizer Pastor Terry Teykl told me. When God put on his heart the burden to build a praying church, he wanted to set aside a prayer room where people could gather any time during the week exclusively for prayer. He found a small room in his church that was full of junk. He was convinced he had found a perfect location for his prayer room. He brought the matter to his board, and to his amazement he was met with significant resistance. After an hour of fruitless discussion, one of his board members raised his arms in frustration and said, "Pastor, if we give you that room for prayer, what in the world are we going to do with our junk?" When the man realized what he had said, everyone burst out laughing. It is a sad day, however, when we memorialize our junk and marginalize prayer.

Perhaps the most dramatic example of Christ's anger was when He cleaned out the temple and demanded that His house become a house of prayer. That same Jesus will help you clean your church calendar so that you can get rid of your junk and give priority to prayer.

When I lived in South Florida as a young man, I got hooked on saltwater game fishing—snook, redfish, trout, tarpon, shark and cobia were my favorite. Very early one morning when my alarm went off at zero-dark-thirty, I jumped up off the mattress and headed for my fishing pole. A thought went through my mind as if God was speaking to me, *Why aren't you this excited to meet with Me?* God stopped me in my tracks. I knew it was the voice of the Holy Spirit. I felt as if I had been hit in the head with a fifty-pound tuna! I sat down and repented. I was legitimately convicted that I had gotten so caught up with the thrill of a fish that I might not even catch and had utterly neglected the thrill of a sure thing: meeting with Christ and encountering His manifest presence. I put my pole back in the closet and got my Bible. This began a whole new pattern of early rising for me.

Ever since that moment as a young man, I have made a habit of setting an appointment to meet with God. If anyone asks to meet with me during that time slot, I simply say, "I'm sorry. I can't; I already have an appointment."

Now It's Your Turn: Day 8 Action Step

It is important for you to make an appointment to meet with your Father. Give Him the best time at the start of your day. If you are not a morning person, give Him an hour in the evening when you are most clearheaded. Turn off the TV and spend the time alone with God. Jesus said to His disciples, "Could you men not keep watch with me for one hour? . . . Watch and pray" (Matt. 26:40–41). This certainly suggests that an hour with Him is a baseline.

So what time will it be for you to meet with God? Get out your calendar now and schedule your appointment with Him.

Lord Jesus, what You are teaching me today is _____

_____

Lord Jesus, the action step that I will take is _____

_____

Day 9

SADDLE UP

The best way to learn to pray is to pray with people who know how to pray. Let me encourage you: right now there are people around you who are waiting for you to invite them into an entry-level prayer partnership.

When God first put me under orders in the vise grip of prayer with a desire to learn to pray and to bring people with me, I didn't know exactly where to start, but I figured that I could not go wrong inviting three people whom I knew had a prayer life to pray with me: Don, Leslie and Daniel. Don works for FedEx, Leslie is a massage therapist par excellence and Daniel works for Home Depot. Along with a few others, we became a small core prayer group. Our backgrounds could not have been more diverse, but that didn't matter because our hearts were together—we each loved Jesus and wanted Him to teach us to pray.

I have grown tremendously from my mentors—Armin Gesswein, David Bryant, Henry Blackaby and Victor Hashweh—but these relationships have been long distance. I've been profoundly impacted by Jim Cymbala, Richard Foster, Alice Smith and other prayer leaders, but that has been primarily through casual friendships and books. The number of my intercessors has grown over the years, and our prayer team has changed, but without question I have learned more about prayer and advancing Christ's kingdom from kneeling with my three trusted prayer partners, with whom I saddled up as in a posse fifteen years ago, than from anyone else on earth. We have been riding together ever since those early days. The *Urban Dictionary* defines posse as "your crew, your homies, a group of friends, people who have your back";[1] we might define it as "your entry-level core prayer partners."

Jesus' Method

Jesus spent three years making upper-room disciples. We know that He practiced a life of prayer: "Very early in the morning, while it was still dark, Jesus got up, left the house and went off to a solitary place, where he prayed" (Mark 1:35). He also modeled a lifestyle of prayer for His disciples. Even in the middle of heavy days of nonstop ministry to needy people, Jesus called time-out: "Jesus often withdrew to lonely places and prayed" (Luke 5:16). His example of relevant, life-giving prayer was so winsome to His disciples that one day, after Jesus finished praying, "one of his disciples said to him, 'Lord, teach us to pray, just as John taught his disciples'" (Luke 11:1). Normally, we ask people to teach us what they are best at. When we stop to consider the fact that Jesus was good at so many things—teaching, preaching, healing, casting out demons, making disciples—it is worth noting that the only thing His disciples asked Him to teach them was to pray. It may be fair to assume that Jesus was more alive, more adept, more Himself, more vibrant and infectious when He prayed than when He was doing anything else.

Jesus took His disciples off alone by themselves for the single, express purpose of praying. "Jesus . . . took Peter, John and James with him and went up onto a mountain to pray" (Luke 9:28). When Jesus made disciples, He made praying disciples, and He set the model for the rest of us.

Pray Now

When Christ sets off our spiritual appetite alarm, we immediately and instinctively want to pray with others. Many of us were raised in the generation that was taught solo prayer—to pray in private. Many grew up in a church in which the corporate prayer meeting was dry, irrelevant and boring. I must admit that I have suffered through plenty of boring— painfully boring—prayer meetings. They were torturous for only one reason: they lacked the fire of God's manifest presence.

Once God has stirred a passion in us to pray and to receive the fire of His manifest presence, it is an indication that He has also stirred a similar passion in others around us. I have found that this is virtually a universal principle that we can count on. It's just a matter of discovering who these people are. God will help us identify them and gather them in prayer.

My friend and mentor J. Edwin Orr was not only a brilliant revival historian with three earned doctorates in the history of revival, he was also a catalytic practitioner who was anointed to stir people to seek Christ and to gather them in God-encountering prayer. As a young man desperate for God, I attended a conference on revival prayer at which Dr. Orr was a speaker. My friends and I took him out to lunch and asked him, "In your sixty years of study, can you summarize everything you've learned in a single sentence?" I waited to hear his next comment.

"Yes," the great revival Jedi-master replied. "Whenever God is ready to begin something new with His people, He always sets them to praying."[2]

This single summary statement is profound. Noteworthy are its two main points: God always goes first, and He does so by mobilizing corporate prayer.

This principle that Dr. Orr clarified is rooted in one of Jesus' favorite promises: "These I will bring to my holy mountain and give them joy in my house of prayer. . . . For my house will be called a house of prayer for all nations" (Isa. 56:7).

Did you notice again that it is God who goes first and that He goes first by gathering His people in corporate prayer? Prayer is God's primary work that will characterize the gathering of His people.

Don't you love that the dominant characteristic of the atmosphere of the God-encountering house of prayer is joy? I frequently tell my prayer leaders, "Lead with joy!" When Christ is out front leading the prayer meeting, we are free to be ourselves and to encourage everyone else to be themselves. When the Holy Spirit is running the prayer meeting and we follow His leadership, there will always be an atmosphere of freedom and joy.

Now It's Your Turn: Day 9 Action Step

You don't need to be a pastor to gather a core of praying people. Everyone wants to have a huge prayer gathering like Pastor Jim Cymbala's at the Brooklyn Tabernacle, but why not start small? Give God time to lay a solid foundation with a core group. In the weeks to come, you will have opportunity with the full support and blessing of your lead pastor to launch a church-wide, God-encountering prayer gathering, but gather your core prayer friends now.

Start by asking the Lord, "Father, who would You have me invite into an entry-level prayer partnership?" He will tell you. Write down your initial prospect list below. It's time for you to form your posse and saddle up.

_____   _____

_____   _____

_____   _____

_____   _____

- Set a date and time to launch your God-encountering prayer gathering for your core praying friends. To do this, ask God, "Lord, what is the best time to meet?" Feel free to call your prospect list of core prayer partners and ask them what the best time slot is for them. Set the date and time for your initial meeting.

- Set the location.

- Invite your people. Start small with your prospect list of core prayer partners.

- Keep your meeting simple. Lead with joy. Give people freedom to pray. Worship first. Sing. Announce to your group, "If you have a prayer, pray it. If you have a song, sing it, and if we know it, we will sing with you. If you have a scripture, read it."

- Pray with your core group for protection, direction and revelation. We have discovered that these three prayers, while certainly not a magic formula, are biblical, strategic and significant. (1) *Protection*. One-third of the Psalms are prayers for protection. We need protection because the enemy is about to lose ground rapidly, and we do not want his interference. We want to proactively dismantle his activity at the outset. (2) *Direction*. We sincerely and legitimately rely on Holy Spirit direction in our gathering. (3) *Revelation*. We want Christ to reveal Himself, and we need the Holy Spirit's help in that process. Paul very clearly prayed for this: "I keep asking that the God of our Lord Jesus Christ, the glorious Father, may give you the Spirit of wisdom and revelation, so that you may know him better" (Eph. 1:17).

Don't be afraid to start small. Jesus started with twelve, and at times He limited His prayer team to only three. The great revivalist prophet Zechariah was one of Jonathan Edwards' favorite prophets. Zechariah asked the relevant revival question, "Who despises the day of small things?" (Zech. 4:10). Jesus even defended small things and small beginnings when He said of the kingdom of God, "It is like a mustard seed, which is the smallest seed you plant in the ground. Yet when planted, it grows and becomes the largest of all garden plants, with such big branches that the birds of the air can perch in its shade" (Mark 4:31–32).

Lord Jesus, what You are teaching me today is _____

_____

Lord Jesus, the action step that I will take is _____

_____

Day 10

AGREE TOGETHER

The first miracle that Christ performs in any local church is the formation of the church itself. Gathering people together from a range of backgrounds and uniting them in Christ is indeed a miraculous accomplishment of extraordinary proportion. On the surface it may appear that church is what we do, but underneath the surface the gathering together of believers is 100 percent what God does. Until we recognize the miracle of the gathering, we will always mess it up.

One of the reasons that our concept of church is skewed is because when we think "church," we think "building." Wrong. Church is not a physical structure but a relational gathering together. The word Jesus used for "church" was *ekklesia*, which means "called out and called together."[1] The first time Jesus used the word, He said, "I will build my church [*ekklesia*], and the gates of hell shall not prevail against it" (Matt. 16:18, ESV). This gathering, or building, of people together in public, corporate assembly is no minor miracle. Jesus built the early church, and Jesus Himself is right now leveraging the entire weight of His leadership influence in gathering your church and mine. This is what some refer to as "gathering-anointing."

The only other time Jesus uses the word *ekklesia* is found two chapters later in Matthew 18:17. He takes the principle of *ekklesia* to the next level by giving the disciples the kingdom principle of the power of agreement:

> I tell you the truth, whatever you bind on earth will be bound in heaven, and whatever you loose on earth will be loosed in heaven. Again, I tell you that if two of you on earth agree about anything you ask for, it will be done for you by my Father in heaven. (18:18–19)

The power of agreement is not simply a minor side benefit for the church to enjoy; it is actually a major purpose for which the church exists—in order to advance Christ's kingdom on earth and to overthrow enemy forces. For this reason Christ has given us authority to bind and to loose. Too many Christians try to make binding and loosing far too complicated. Jesus didn't elaborate on the terms because He didn't need to. Very simply, we have been empowered to bind what is evil and to loose what is good, to exercise authority in corporate prayer and in declarations of agreement. Allow me to provide a few examples of what we bind and what we loose:

Bind	Loose
Fear	Courage
Poverty	Provision
Violence	Peace
Sickness	Health
Deception	Truth
Darkness	Light
Bondage	Freedom
Confusion	Clarity
Foolishness	Wisdom
Unbelief	Faith
Hate	Love
Unforgiveness	Forgiveness

Unhindered Prayers

If you sincerely intend to build a God-encountering, praying church and to bring others along with you, you want to first learn to bind and loose at home. God wants to release His manifest presence in your marriage and in your family, and this begins when you start to consistently pray with your spouse.

When Jerry walked into the night of prayer at our church, it was obvious he had a heavy heart. He explained that his dad had just been diagnosed with terminal cancer and given only a few months to live. Then he told me the worst news as he broke down crying: "Pastor, my dad is not a Christian." I felt the weight of his burden. Though Jerry had attempted many times to share the good news of Christ with his dad, his father had remained disinterested. He and I stopped immediately to pray for his dad. As we did, the Lord said to me, "Bind the enemy; Satan is blinding his eyes." I thought immediately of the scripture, "The god of this age has blinded the minds of unbelievers, so that they cannot see the light of the gospel of the glory of Christ, who is the image of God" (2 Cor. 4:4).

We stopped praying, and I led Jerry to bind Satan from his father: "Satan, I bind you right now in the name of the Lord Jesus Christ. I command you to go from Jerry's dad, for it is written, 'Resist the devil, and he will flee from you' (James 4:7). I forbid you from blinding his eyes any longer, and you cannot prevent him from receiving salvation in the Lord Jesus Christ." Then we prayed, "Father, we declare that this is the day of salvation for Jerry's dad. Send the Holy Spirit to him now so that he will come to know eternal life through Christ alone." As soon as we stopped praying, God gave me a strategy to use to share the good news of Christ with Jerry's dad. Jerry and I followed the strategy, and two weeks later I called his dad on the phone, and he prayed with me to receive Christ. A month later he was baptized, and three months later he was in heaven. Don't underestimate the effectiveness of binding Satan. I can tell you dozens of similar stories of friends, family and neighbors who have come to know Christ after my wife and I exercised our authority in binding and loosing.

Agreeing at Home

The apostle Peter gave some of the all-time best marriage advice:

> Husbands, in the same way be considerate as you live with your wives, and treat them with respect as the weaker partner and as heirs with you of the gracious gift of life, so that nothing will hinder your prayers. (1 Pet. 3:7)

If the verse said "so your sex lives would not be hindered," we would all perk up, listen and pay close attention. The highest value of marriage, however, is not a sexual encounter but a spiritual encounter with our God. We as spouses love each other, bless each other and honor each other so that we might reach the higher purpose of encountering the manifest presence of Christ together.

After eleven years of marriage, I came home one evening and told Sherry that after we ate and put the kids to bed, I had a surprise for her. When the kids were all tucked in, we sat on the couch, and I began, "Would you forgive me for not being the spiritual leader in our marriage?" She was touched, and she freely forgave me.

"I want to make a commitment to you," I said as her eyes began to moisten. "I want to begin praying with you every day." She started to cry for joy. She had been patiently waiting for this moment for many years. She had gently and respectfully asked me to pray with her since we were first married, and I had casually and condescendingly dismissed the request as a wife's whim. I didn't know why, but I had never taken it seriously. In fact, to be even more vulnerable, the thought of praying consistently with Sherry was actually intimidating to me. I had a long list of reasons as to why I—and many husbands—freak out when we think about praying with our wives.[2] But that day everything changed in my heart. I bellied up to the fact that my pride was at the root of my problem. I humbled myself with Sherry and asked her to forgive me. I replaced my prideful resistance with humility and prayer.

That day both my marriage and my life changed. By the grace of God, I can report to you that we just celebrated our fortieth wedding anniversary, and Sherry and I have prayed together virtually every day since I first humbled myself. For almost thirty years now, we have enjoyed countless benefits of agreeing together in prayer. Here are several:

- *Power of agreement.* Jesus said, "If two of you on earth agree about anything you ask for, it will be done for you by my Father in heaven" (Matt. 18:19). It does not take long to agree together in prayer. I can get a faster answer to a five-second prayer with Sherry than I can by praying for an hour without her.

- *Victory over anger.* Paul said, "Do not let the sun go down while you are still angry, and do not give the devil a foothold" (Eph. 4:26–27). There is no way that we can pray when we are angry. The commitment to pray together every day with our spouse keeps us from allowing the devil to get a foothold in our relationship.

- *The manifest presence of Christ.* "Where two or three come together in my name, there am I with them" (Matt. 18:20). The greatest benefit of agreeing together is that we get to welcome the manifest presence of Christ into our lives and marriage every day.

Once a week or so, Sherry and I enjoy an extended time of prayer for fifteen minutes to an hour or more, but normally, we only pray together for a minute or two each day. We alternate—some nights she prays, and some nights I pray. If I am too tired as we lie in bed, I tap her leg and ask her to pray. If she's too tired, she taps me back. Some nights when we both feel exhausted, we pray unusually brief prayers. On one memorable night I dug deep, and with all the energy I could muster, I simply said, "Goodnight, God!"

You may think that this is silly or even legalistic. Not at all. Legalism is being forced to do something that you don't want to do or thinking that when you do it, you are better than others. Praying daily with Sherry is what I want to do, not something I have to do. It doesn't make me feel better than anyone else, but I am certainly thankful for all its benefits.

Part of the beauty of agreement is that it doesn't take long. We can agree in one second. Binding and loosing is the same way. We don't need to pray for hours to bind and loose—it can be done in a few seconds. *Father, I bind_____ in the name of the Lord Jesus Christ. I loose _____.* You can't beat that!

Now It's Your Turn: Day 10 Action Step

The power of agreement is a blessing you can begin using now. Use the authority of binding and loosing with your prayer group. Sometimes it is also important to be able to agree with just one trusted friend. If you are single, with whom do you want to start a prayer partnership—someone you trust with whom you can share deep, personal needs and agree together in prayer? Invite that person to be your prayer partner. If you are married, your spouse is your ready-made prayer partner. If you have not yet made a commitment to pray with your spouse every day, you don't know what you are missing. Humble yourself. Go to your spouse, and share your desire to begin praying every day. Make the commitment. Start today.

Lord Jesus, what You are teaching me today is _____

_____

Lord Jesus, the action step that I will take is _____

_____

Week 2: Questions for Small Groups

1. Have someone in your group read aloud Acts 1:1–14. What impact did Jesus' command "Do not leave Jerusalem" have on the early disciples? What significant kingdom principle do these four words teach us?

2. What does it mean to "minister to the Lord"? Be specific. Why is this our first assignment?

3. There are three examples in Scripture of individuals who were people of *one thing*: David in Psalm 27:4, Mary in Luke 10:41–42 and Paul in Philippians 3:13–14. Using your own words, how would you describe a person of *one thing*?

4. What are the five characteristics of the upper room that correspond to the five aspects of every room: door, atmosphere, walls, floor and ceiling?

5. For you to be an upper-room disciple, what walls will you personally need to erect to protect your schedule and allow for extended times of prayer and corporate prayer?

6. Have you ever had a prayer partner with whom you met consistently to seek the face of Christ? Describe the benefits you experienced. Who in your life right now do you think has a hunger for God whom you might consider inviting into a prayer partnership?

7. What impresses you most about Jesus' prayer life? Why? Be specific.

8. Describe what we mean by spiritual hunger and spiritual appetite. On a scale of one to ten, how would you rank your own spiritual hunger? Why? The hunger of your church family?

9. Jesus tells us the power of agreement in prayer. Read Matthew 18:18–20. Why do you think that agreement is so effective?

10. Have you ever considered praying daily with your spouse? What are some of the obvious benefits you might receive?

Week 2: Advice for Pastors

As the gatekeeper in your local church, you are learning what it means to minister to the presence of the Lord. How is it going? With all the demands of church work that require public ministry, God wants to empower you to take dominion over your schedule as you come under orders to pray first. Right now God wants to empower you to rebuild your own heart to seek first Christ and His kingdom and to clear your personal calendar before you try to clear your church calendar. Only then can you recruit a few other Christ seekers to saddle up with you.

Pastors' wives can be the most lonely, neglected people in the entire congregation. With the overwhelming demands of ministry in the twenty-first century, today is a perfect opportunity for you to call time-out, sit with your wife, ask her heart questions, listen to her and make a commitment to be her spiritual leader. Humble yourself. Tell your wife that your first and most important public ministry is to her and that everyone else comes second. Commit yourself, by the grace of God, to pray with her every day.

If you have chosen to go through this thirty-one-day adventure corporately, it will be helpful for you at this point in your journey to share with your congregation one specific blessing that you have already received during the adventure.

WELCOME THE FIRE

What separates our church from the sports bar or the health club down the street is not the omnipresence of God. It may sound crude, but the omnipresence of God is as much at the gay bar downtown as it is at First Baptist or Willow Creek. What distinguishes the church from any other institution on earth is the flaming reality of the manifest presence of Christ.

A church without the manifest presence of Christ is not a church—it's a knockoff. A car without an engine is not a car—it's a chassis. A church without the manifest presence of Christ is not a church—it's a club.

The reason young adults are leaving the church in droves is because, if they want a club, they can find something more exciting. It is time for us not only to rediscover the distinction between the omnipresence of God and His manifest presence; it is time for us to lead our people back to encounter the manifest presence of Christ.

Week three is the critical week of our thirty-one-day adventure. This is the week we move from talking about the fire to actually receiving the fire. Ready or not, church on fire, here we come.

Day 11

Don't Fear the Fire

If the primary purpose of the church was to hold out propositional truth, Jesus might have been seen walking in a library. If the church was ultimately a preaching center, He might have walked among the lecterns, soapboxes or pulpits. If the purpose of the church was primarily to deploy troops on a mission for Christ, Jesus might have walked on the deck of an aircraft carrier. If the purpose of the church was primarily to treat the wounded, He might have been walking the halls of a hospital.[1] When John saw the exalted, enthroned Christ in the first chapter of the book of the Revelation, however, the Lord was walking among the flame holders. Each flame holder represented a different local church during the first century in what is now the western half of Turkey. These same flame holders show us that the primary purpose of the church is to hold out the fire of the manifest presence of God.

Why Fire?

The first glimpse we have of the early church is of the church in the fire. On the day of Pentecost, the early church was baptized in the Holy Spirit and fire. Not surprisingly, the head of every believer in the building was covered with what literally looked like flames (see Acts 2:3).

The final picture we have of the early church is also of the church in the fire. When the risen, ascended, exalted and enthroned Christ revealed Himself to the apostle John, who was serving time as a political prisoner of Rome exiled on the Mediterranean island of Patmos, John saw fire. As Christ is portrayed walking among the seven churches in the book of the Revelation, each church is not only on fire—it is actually a holder of the flame. When John the apostle turned around to see the voice of the One speaking to him, he first saw the flame holders (see Rev. 1:12).

Think of it—flame holders define the essence of the church. The Greek word for flame holder is *luxnos*; what John saw were seven free-standing pieces of furniture that held oil that were ignited to provide light to those in their vicinity. The *luxnos* was not the flame, but it carried the flame. This flaming image provides a profound prophetic picture of the essential identity of the church as an entity that holds out the flame of God's manifest presence to the world. As a *luxnos* exists for the sole purpose of extending light, so the church exists for the single purpose of holding out the flame of God's manifest presence. There is no other human institution that can fulfill this unique role. *Church on fire* is a fitting description of the reason that the church exists on earth.

The apostle John explained, "I turned around to see the voice that was speaking to me. And when I turned I saw seven golden lampstands [*luxnos*], and among the lampstands [*luxnos*] was someone 'like a son of man'" (Rev. 1:12–13). Christ is still walking among the lampstands. He is inspecting the flame, expecting your church and mine to hold out the raging inferno of the manifest presence of Christ.

The single reason that your church is in your community is to hold out the manifest presence of Christ. This means that Christ wants to visit your church family in tangible ways that even your unchurched neighbors can understand.

From the first picture we have of the New Testament church in the upper room on the day of Pentecost to the final picture of the church on Patmos, we have the same message: the church is here on earth to carry the fire—the fire of the manifest presence of Christ. Fire is not human passion or enthusiasm. Neither is it religious activity. Fire is not our activity but God's. Fire is the manifest presence of Christ.

Fire Manifestations

The Bible is full of God-encountering fire manifestations. Think about it.

God revealed Himself in the bush on fire to Moses, because He wanted Moses to lead His people out of slavery into the Promised Land (see Exod. 3:2).

God wanted to turn His people from idols to serve the living God, so Elijah boldly declared, "The God who answers by fire—he is God" (1 Kings 18:24). When Elijah prayed, fire fell from heaven, and the people fell flat on their faces in worship (see 18:36–39).

When Solomon completed the temple, God wanted to lead His people beyond mere external worship into wholehearted worship, so He poured out fire to consume the massive offering of animals and filled the temple with His glory (see 2 Chron. 6:1–7:10).

God took a flaming coal from the altar and touched Isaiah's lips, because He wanted to raise up a prophetic voice to turn His people back to Himself (see Isa. 6:6–7).

God filled the church with His Holy Spirit and covered each person with what looked like flames of fire when He gave birth to the church and empowered the church to make disciples of all nations (see Acts 2:3–4).

God showed the apostle John the final picture of the church in the Bible by revealing the dramatic picture of lampstands, or holders of fire (see Rev. 1:12).

It is not surprising that Paul exhorted the believers in the church in the city of Thessalonica, "Do not put out the Spirit's fire" (1 Thess. 5:19).

In each of these examples, fire represented the manifest presence of God. God was the focus, not the fire. No one began worshiping fire; they began to worship God. It is important for us to keep in mind that most often the manifest presence of God will not be accompanied by fire, at least not literal fire. The critical issue is not the perception of fire but the presence of God. It is important for us to keep our focus on Christ and not on the manifestation. At the same time, it is important for us to recognize not only that there is such a thing as the manifest presence of Christ but that His manifest presence plays an irreplaceable role in the church.

All-Important Difference

The tragedy of the modern church is that we have settled for the omnipresence of God and virtually overlooked the manifest presence of God. Don't misunderstand me—the omnipresence of God is a profound reality. The fact that God is everywhere at the same time present, that He promises never to leave us or forsake us (see Heb. 13:5), that He is with us wherever we go (see Josh. 1:9), that He is with us always (see Matt. 28:20), that it is impossible to hide from His Spirit (see Ps. 139:7–8) is not only biblical but comforting and beneficial. We must realize, however, that we can't get any more or less of His omnipresence—that His omnipresence benefits all people equally, whether it be Hindus, Buddhists, Muslims, Jews, secular atheists or Christians. For this reason the omnipresence of God requires absolutely no prayer. There is no need for us to ever ask for God's omnipresence.

The manifest presence of God, however, is categorically different. By definition, God's manifest presence is impossible to miss. Unlike His omnipresence, God's manifest presence is selective and highly personal. A.W. Tozer was a forerunner in prayer who pointed out that there is a Grand Canyon difference between the two: "The presence and the manifest presence are not the same. There can be one without the other. God is here when we are wholly unaware of it. He is manifest only when and as we are aware of His presence."[2] While there is no need to ask for God's omnipresence, encountering His manifest presence is at the very heart of prayer. It may be helpful to compare and contrast the distinction between the omnipresence of God and His manifest presence:

Omnipresence	Manifest Presence
Biblical	Biblical
Real	Real
True to God's nature	True to God's nature
God is everywhere	God is tangibly perceived
Generally theoretical	Generally transformational
Available to all	Normally for God's people
Universal	Selective
Generally impersonal	Highly personal
Abstract	Specific
Obedience rare	Obedience required
Absolutely no prayer required	Normally prayer required[3]

Now It's Your Turn: Day 11 Action Step

It is quite possible that your church family today does not conspicuously resemble a flame holder. You may not see it that way, but God does. Perhaps your entire church experience, even the church you grew up in, might have been boring, predictable and forgettable, not at all a flame holder in which you encountered the manifest presence of Christ. Jesus has a different perspective as to what your church should be. Today, agree with God's perspective, and start to see your church as a flame holder. In the space following, using simple words or phrases, describe what it would look like for the manifest presence of Christ to fill your Sunday morning worship.

_____

_____

_____

Lord Jesus, what You are teaching me today is _____

_____

Lord Jesus, the action step that I will take is _____

_____

Day 12

Pray Your Hunger

Welcoming the fire of God's manifest presence is not complicated. We don't need a twelve-step program on how to set our church on fire. We can heave a big sigh of relief because fire is God's work, not ours. All we need to do is pray our hunger and gather hungry people to pray with us.

If Anyone Is Thirsty

Praying our spiritual hunger is the key to every revival. Jesus set this principle in motion in a booming voice to a crowd of "wannabe" worshipers:

> On the last and greatest day of the Feast, Jesus stood and said in a loud voice, "If a man is thirsty, let him come to me and drink. Whoever believes in me, as the Scripture has said, streams of living water will flow from within him." By this he meant the Spirit, whom those who believed in him were later to receive. (John 7:37–39)

I love the fact that Jesus made this statement in a loud voice. I guess He wanted everyone to hear it. In a sense His words are still echoing through the ages of revival church history. The Welsh revivalist Evan Roberts loved these words of Jesus and used them as the catalyst of a profound move of the Holy Spirit that ran throughout the British Isles. In only six months of ministry, one hundred thousand people came to Christ during the Welsh revival.[1] When the Holy Spirit comes, God can accomplish more in a day than we can in a year or even a lifetime.

Christian leaders throughout the ages have cried out to God for fire. Charles Spurgeon, perhaps the most quoted preacher in history, longed for the fire. "The kingdom comes not and the work is flagging. Oh, that You would send the wind and the fire," he preached.[2] Henry Martyn, pioneer missionary to India and Iran, longed for the fire. "Let me burn out for God," he cried.[3] Jim Elliot, pioneer missionary to Ecuador, longed for the fire. "Saturate me with the oil of your Spirit that I may be aflame," he prayed.[4] Samuel Chadwick, a Spirit-filled Wesleyan Methodist minister and author, longed for the fire. "The sign of Christianity is not a cross, but a tongue of fire," he wrote.[5] William Booth, founder of the Salvation

Army, longed for the fire. He wrote in a hymn, "Thou Christ of burning, cleansing flame. Send the fire, send the fire, send the fire!" Christmas Evans, the great Welsh leader, longed for the fire. "Revival is God bending down to the dying embers of a fire just about to go out and breathing into it until it bursts into flames," he declared.[6] Oswald Chambers, the inspirational author, longed for the fire. "The Holy Spirit must anoint me for the work, fire me, and so vividly convince me that such and such a way is mine to aim at, or I shall not go, I will not, I dare not. . . . Nothing but the fire of the most Holy Spirit of God can make the offering holy and unblameable and acceptable in his sight."[7] Smith Wigglesworth, the great Pentecostal forerunner, longed for the fire. "A flame of fire! It is a perpetual fire; a constant fire; a continual burning; a holy, inward flame; which is exactly what God's Son was in the world. God has nothing less for us than to be flames!"[8]

Longing for Fire Today

God is kindling a new heart cry for a fresh baptism of the fire of the manifest presence of Christ in the church today. Nothing more vividly demonstrates this than the lyrics of our current songwriters. Tim Hughes sings, "Consuming fire, fan into flame a passion for Your name."[9] The Rend Collective Experiment sings, "Like wildfire in our very souls, Holy Spirit come invade us now."[10] Brooke Fraser sings, "I see the King of glory coming on the clouds with fire."[11] Jesus Culture sings, "Set a fire down in my soul that I can't contain and I can't control. I want more of You, God,"[12] and again in their song "Show Me Your Glory," they sing, "I want to walk in Your presence."[13] Christy Nockels sings, "Our God is a consuming fire, a burning holy flame, with glory and freedom."[14] Hillsong sings, "As we seek, Your fire fall down, fire fall down on us, we pray."[15] When Jeremy Riddle sings, "Yes, Spirit, come and fill this place," he is not asking for the omnipresence; he wants the manifest presence of Christ.[16] In his song "Better Is One Day," Matt Redman sings, "Here my heart is satisfied within Your presence."[17]

What level of spiritual hunger is God creating in you and in your church family?

As you pray your hunger, don't seek an experience; seek an encounter with Christ. What's the difference? An experience puts the focus on you; an encounter puts the focus on Christ. An experience is something that makes us want to keep the horse in front of the cart, but when we seek an encounter with the manifest presence of Christ, we turn our eyes away from ourselves, put them on Christ and pray our hunger. "If anyone is thirsty"—does that describe you? Then keep it simple and do what the rest of the verse says: "Come to me and drink" (John 7:37). Drinking is receiving.

Now It's Your Turn: Day 12 Action Step

When Jesus wanted to set the first church on fire, He gave them a command and a promise. The command was that they were to gather, and the promise was that they would receive. Jesus repeated the promise on numerous occasions. Just as we don't baptize ourselves but rather wade into the waters for the pastor to immerse us, so Jesus is the baptizer, or immerser, in the Holy Spirit. He is the one who fills us. Allow the Holy Spirit to take you beneath the surface with God. Jesus gave us promises so that we might believe them, pray them and receive from Him their fulfillment:

> Do not leave Jerusalem, but wait for the gift my Father promised, which you have heard me speak about. For John baptized with water, but in a few days you will be baptized with the Holy Spirit. (Acts 1:4–5)

> You will receive power when the Holy Spirit comes on you; and you will be my witnesses in Jerusalem, and in all Judea and Samaria, and to the ends of the earth. (1:8)

> Receive the Holy Spirit. (John 20:22)

> I am going to send you what my Father has promised; but stay in the city until you have been clothed with power from on high. (Luke 24:49)

Take time right now to reword these promises as prayer. Don't just pray—receive.

Lord Jesus, what You are teaching me today is _____

_____

Lord Jesus, the action step that I will take is _____

_____

Day 13

GIVE AWAY CONTROL

Welcoming the fire of God's manifest presence sounds intimidating—even threatening. I would dare to say that if the thought of God setting your church on fire does not strike a healthy degree of fear in your bones, I seriously question whether or not you understand it.

It is no mere coincidence that the vast majority of "fear nots" in the Bible were spoken to people who had just encountered the manifest presence of God. When Abraham encountered God in the flaming vision, he was petrified. God was bringing Abraham's control issues to the surface, and He said to him, "Fear not" (see Gen. 15:1). When Daniel encountered the manifest presence of God and the muscle-bound angel, he was overwhelmed. God settled him down by saying, "Fear not" (see Dan. 10:12). When the apostle John encountered the manifest presence of the exalted Christ, the apostle was not sure whether or not he would live through the encounter. God told him, "Fear not" (see Rev. 1:17).

All kinds of scary thoughts race through our mind when we consider welcoming the fire to our church. *What if things get out of hand? If people get carried away? If things get messy? What if people get turned off and leave my church?*

Some of us are so afraid of false fire misfire or backfire that when things start to heat up, we panic and instinctively reach for the fire extinguishers. One of my admired pastor friends Erwin McManus exposes our controlling instinct when he writes, "Sometimes we forget that God is fire. We confuse Him with fireplaces and fireworks."[1] When we try to contain God's fire in a fireplace, we clearly have a control issue.

The question in your church is, does the Holy Spirit control you, or do you control the Holy Spirit? You cannot wholeheartedly welcome the fire without relinquishing control. If you sincerely want the Holy Spirit to take control, you need to give Him control.

How Big Is Your Church?

Many of you are asking yourselves, *Can I trust God enough to give Him freedom to manifest Himself in my church regardless of what it looks like? Am I willing to relinquish control of my church to Christ? Or because of my fear of fire, will I retain control?* These are critical questions, and you need to understand what is at stake when you face them.

As you take time to ponder these searching questions, keep this in mind: if you hold onto your church, it will never get any bigger than you are. You will always limit its potential. If on the other hand you relinquish control to the Holy Spirit, there is no limit to the size and potential of your church.

God has told me on numerous occasions that unless I give Him control, my church will never get any bigger than me. But the moment I give Him control, the church's size, influence and scope are limitless.

People often ask, "Since self-control is the fruit of the Holy Spirit [see Gal. 5:23], how can the spirit of control be evil? Aren't they the same thing?" No. The spirit of control and the fruit of the Holy Spirit, self-control, are actually exact opposites. We are not confronting the fruit of the Holy Spirit; we are confronting the sin of unbroken self-will that is behind the spirit of control. A controlling spirit in a church can destroy a church and dangerously limit Holy Spirit activity. Not until we relinquish control can we truly be filled with the Holy Spirit and come under the influence and control of the Holy Spirit. To be Holy Spirit filled is to be Holy Spirit controlled.

The spirit of control prevents more churches from experiencing the manifest presence of Christ than all the debate over pneumatology, that is, the theology of the Holy Spirit. Most church leaders build a pneumatology to suit their control issues.

God never told anyone to control the church. Lead, shepherd and build the church, yes. These are all sanctioned. But control, no. The spirit of control is witchcraft, pure and simple.[2]

Control is what we do in the absence of the manifest presence of Christ. As leaders, when we intuitively feel the void of God's control, we try to fill it with something that we manufacture. At times our church members will even look to us to control the church when they feel the void of Holy Spirit control. We as leaders must resist the temptation to control, or we will never be able to welcome the manifest presence of Christ. When we welcome the manifest presence of Christ, we will be empowered to evict the spirit of control.

When God asked Moses, "What is that in your hand?" (Exod. 4:2), He was confronting Moses' control issues. Face it. Moses had control issues. In the beginning of his life, when he struck and killed an Egyptian, one of his issues was control. At the end of his life, when he struck the rock rather than speaking to it as God had requested, he was disqualified from entering the Promised Land, and his issue again was control. For God to work mightily through Moses, He needed to gain control. This is an issue God confronts in all His leaders. As long as Moses held the staff, it would never be bigger than Moses. As soon as Moses threw it down, the staff was now out of his control and under the control and influence of the Holy Spirit. Through that piece of wood, God would work miracles.

Now It's Your Turn: Day 13 Action Step

Take time today to write out an "I relinquish control" covenant with God. Don't rush the process. Be as thorough as possible. Ask the Holy Spirit to show you the various parameters of control in your life—your family, your thoughts, your habits, your use of time, your use of money, your job, your career path—and to show you any control issues you may have with them. Print your covenant. Date it. Sign it. Read it out loud to God. Allow a few trusted friends to read it and cosign it. Return to it periodically and reread it.

Lord Jesus, what You are teaching me today is _____

_____

Lord Jesus, the action step that I will take is _____

_____

Day 14

RECEIVE CORPORATELY

Church on fire is a church encountering the manifest presence of Christ, because it is a church filled with the Holy Spirit.

Just as God wants every believer not only to be saved but to know that he or she is saved, so He wants every believer to be filled with the Holy Spirit and to know that he or she is filled with the Holy Spirit. In the same way God wants every local church not only to be filled with the Holy Spirit but to know that it is filled. My generation made the tragic mistake of privatizing prayer to the neglect of the biblical model of corporate prayer, and we privatized the infilling of the Holy Spirit to the neglect of the Bible's model of the corporate infilling of the Holy Spirit. We know that God fills individuals, but we need to rediscover the glorious reality of the corporate infilling of the Holy Spirit.

The Biblical Model

When Jesus first told His upper-room disciples, "Receive the Holy Spirit" (John 20:22), He told them to receive corporately.

When He sent them to the upper room to be filled with the Holy Spirit, He sent them corporately—all 120 of them (see Acts 1:15)!

When He poured out His Holy Spirit on them, He filled them corporately (see 2:3).

When Paul exhorted the church in Ephesus, "Do not get drunk on wine, which leads to debauchery. Instead, be filled with the Spirit" (Eph. 5:18), he exhorted them corporately.

While it is certainly appropriate for us to be filled individually, there is no doubt that the biblical pattern of being filled with the Holy Spirit is to be filled corporately as a church body. So what are we afraid of? Why deny our people the very essence of what the church was made for?

Know for Certain

When the early church was filled with the Holy Spirit on Pentecost, there was no doubt about what had just happened—everyone was filled, and each one knew it (see Acts 2:3-4). Months later, after the release of

Peter and John from prison, when the believers gathered for prayer, once again "they were all filled with the Holy Spirit" (4:31), and they all knew it for certain.

Paul introduced the Ephesian believers to the Holy Spirit. He "placed his hands on them, the Holy Spirit came on them, and they spoke in tongues and prophesied" (19:6). There was no doubt in their minds that they had received the Holy Spirit.

When Count Nicholas Ludwig von Zinzendorf gathered 120 of his German prayer partners into an upper-room prayer meeting on August 13, 1727, they were all filled or baptized in the Holy Spirit. "The whole place was indeed a veritable dwelling of God with men," Zinzendorf wrote, referring to this event as their Pentecost.[1] There was no doubt in their minds that they had all been filled with the Holy Spirit.

William J. Seymour, the great Azusa Street revivalist, led his group to be filled with the Holy Spirit. From 1906 to 1914, they sustained a continuous infilling of the Holy Spirit, during which time their numbers grew from five thousand to fifty thousand and they sent missionaries to Africa, Iceland, China and translated their literature into thirty different languages. Within those eight years, they grew from being a small group in Southern California to having churches in every US city that had a population of three thousand or more. Today, only one-hundred-plus years later, eight hundred million believers around the world are part of this great Pentecostal charismatic movement.[2]

Heating Up in Chile

I preached several years ago in Concepción, Chile, and led those gathered to receive the infilling of the Holy Spirit. I will never forget that night. As I preached, the entire congregation of several hundred people all began groaning together with a deep longing of soul. A corporate weeping started subtly and grew more and more pronounced. As I repeated the four words of Christ in the upper room to His disciples, "Receive the Holy Spirit" (John 20:22), people held their sides, rocked back and forth and writhed in pain as if they were in childbirth. The sanctuary became a birthing room. Before I could finish many were on their feet running to the front, under such conviction that it seemed as though their lives depended on receiving God's Spirit right then. They were hungry to receive the fullness of the Holy Spirit. They responded corporately, and God met them corporately. That night that congregation was immediately and unmistakably filled with the Holy Spirit. There was no doubt that they had received.

Every time God pours out His Holy Spirit on a local church, it will look different. God is a creative God with unlimited diversity. He always knows what is right for each group of believers. It's not our responsibility to determine how God will manifest Himself—it is our responsibility simply to welcome Him and to give Him freedom.

At least once a year I lead our church in Atlanta to corporately receive the infilling of the Holy Spirit during a Sunday worship celebration. Here is what it looks like. Following a biblical message on the person and work of the Holy Spirit, we invite everyone to stand and repeat a prayer similar to this one:

> Heavenly Father, we stand before you in the name of the Lord Jesus Christ. We relinquish the control over our lives and over our congregation to You. We declare our absolute allegiance to Christ, and we present ourselves—spirit, soul and body—under the authority of Christ. Right now we receive the fullness of the Holy Spirit. We welcome You and all Your manifestation gifts. Take control of us. We give You freedom to manifest Your presence in any way You choose so that we might receive Your power to be Your witnesses here in our city and around the world. We receive now the fullness of Your Holy Spirit in the name of the Lord Jesus Christ. Amen.

Let's Review

The critical elements of corporately being filled with the Holy Spirit are simple and biblical:

- *Relinquish control.* One precursor of being filled with the Holy Spirit is surrender—relinquishing control over ourselves and our lives.

- *Receive.* Keep in mind that being filled with the Holy Spirit is something we cannot do ourselves. It's not what we do; it's what God does to us. The words "be filled" (Eph. 5:18) are in the passive voice. Too many believers think that they are filled with the Holy Spirit by simply surrendering. Not true. Until we receive, we are not filled. We don't want to settle for just asking—we want to receive.

- *Believe.* Be sure that you are filled. When you are biblically filled with the Holy Spirit, you will know it with absolutely certainty.

Paul reminded the Christians in Galatia of this all-important element when he asked the rhetorical question, "Did you receive the Spirit by observing the law, or by believing what you heard?" (Gal. 3:2). Every believer in the New Testament who was filled with the Holy Spirit knew for certain that he or she had been filled with the Holy Spirit. God wants to give you and your church family the same assurance today.

- *Be empowered.* It is impossible to be inconspicuously filled with the Holy Spirit. There is no such thing. When you are filled, God will supernaturally manifest His presence all over your life and the life of your church family. This is the essential hallmark of the church. "You will receive power when the Holy Spirit comes on you" (Acts 1:8). Count on it. Sometimes there will be the gift of tongues (see 19:6). Sometimes there will be fire (see 2:3). Sometimes the building in which you meet will shake (see 4:31). We do not determine the manifestation; God does. We do, however, have the biblical basis to expect Christ to conspicuously manifest Himself.

Now It's Your Turn: Day 14 Action Step

The action step today is nothing that any one person or small group can accomplish on its own. In collaboration with your church influencers and certainly under the direction and full blessing of your lead pastor, lead your church toward a corporate gathering in which you as a church family will receive the infilling of the Holy Spirit. Use the model prayer provided earlier in this chapter, or write your own prayer that includes the same biblical elements.

Regardless of the level of influence you have in your church, you can pray in the direction of having an upper-room praying church. You and others in your church can begin praying the following verses, asking God to do today in your church what He did before in the early church:

They saw what seemed to be tongues of fire that separated and came to rest on each of them. All of them were filled with the Holy Spirit and began to speak in other tongues as the Spirit enabled them. (2:3–4)

After they prayed, the place where they were meeting was shaken. And they were all filled with the Holy Spirit and spoke the word of God boldly. (Acts 4:31)

When Paul placed his hands on them, the Holy Spirit came on them, and they spoke in tongues and prophesied. (19:6)

Lord Jesus, what You are teaching me today is _____

_____

Lord Jesus, the action step that I will take is _____

_____

Day 15

KEEP YOUR EYES ON JESUS

The single distinguishing mark of a Holy Spirit-filled congregation is its unmistakable love of Jesus. When a church family is filled with the Holy Spirit, both casual conversations and worship songs will center on Jesus. The presence of Christ will infiltrate not only Sunday worship but also family life, business, pleasure, hobbies, TV viewing, Friday nights, sports, recreation, friendships and spare time. Even our money trail will reflect our love and devotion for Christ. Show me a congregation filled with the Holy Spirit, and I will show you a bunch of people who are head over heels in love with Jesus.

First Things First

When we and our people are first filled with the Holy Spirit, and God begins to manifest Himself among us, there is a temptation to shift the focus away from Christ and onto the manifestations. Rather than explaining this distinction, allow me to illustrate it.

The believers in Jerusalem today can outpray any church I know of on earth. I have been in over forty nations and prayed with thousands of different congregations, and I can honestly say that the focus, zeal, desperation and integrity of the church in Jerusalem are unusual. These believers set the pace for the rest of us.

In August 2013 when the College of Prayer met with the church leaders in Bethlehem for our four-day module in the Holy Land, our meetings started at nine in the morning and continued until nine at night with only a ninety-minute break for both lunch and dinner. That would normally have been more than enough prayer, worship, preaching and teaching for even the best of us, but not for them. They met again at ten for prayer and worship that often lasted until two in the morning. Even in the wee hours of the night, the intensity of zeal and worship were as high-pitched as it had been first thing in the morning. As if that were not enough, they then got up at five and enjoyed two more hours of extra-curricular praise and worship before breakfast! No one forced any of them to stay up late or get up early or told them they should call for these extra worship times. No one. They were there for one reason: they loved Jesus, and they were hungry for more of Him.

When I was told, immediately prior to the morning session I was scheduled to teach, about all this extra prayer and worship, I thought to myself, *They must be exhausted! They will probably drag themselves in here late and have little or nothing to give today. They will be a bunch of sleepy people!* To my utter amazement they were more fervent, zealous and wholehearted in worship that day than ever before.

I have learned so much from the members of the church in Jerusalem. I have worshiped in their building near the Via Dolorosa. I have visited them at their businesses within the Old City. I have eaten their delicious hummus in their homes. I have attended their schools and ridden in their cars. I can assure you that for them, worshiping Jesus is not something they turn on and off—it is a lifestyle. They talk about Jesus when they worship, when they play, when they do business, in their homes and throughout their day. And it is all done in a most natural and authentic manner.

What you also need to know is that virtually all the manifestation gifts are active among them. They have the gifts of the Holy Spirit in full operation: prophecy, tongues and interpretation, words of wisdom, words of knowledge, discernment of spirits, miracles and faith (see 1 Cor. 12). They frequently have God-given dreams and visions and many miraculous healings. One dear pastor's wife was miraculously healed one evening of chronic headaches, and her leg, which had been shorter than the other since birth, was instantly lengthened. I don't mean to freak you out, but when I was with them, someone laid my hands prayerfully on a believer who instantly flew eight feet across the room under the power of the Holy Spirit. (Yes, this person was completely unharmed—in fact, he reported that he had never felt better in his life!) The reason I tell you about all these Holy Spirit manifestations is to point out that while all this supernatural power is being demonstrated among them on a daily basis, they are not distracted by it. Jesus is the big deal among them, not the manifestations.

The church in Jerusalem enjoys a wonderful freedom from so many of the cultural religious entanglements that other congregations seem unable to escape. They welcome the manifest presence of Christ, and they give God freedom to manifest Himself in any way He chooses. Because of their receptivity, God is able to do mighty things among them. At the same time, they keep the main thing the main thing. They refreshingly keep their eyes on Jesus. They worship the Giver, not the gifts. They celebrate the presence, not the presents.

Jesus said in reference to the Holy Spirit, "He will testify about me" (John 15:26), and, "He will bring glory to me by taking from what is mine and making it known to you" (16:14). I love the words of respected Bible teacher F.B. Meyer, who underscores this important principle:

> He is like a shaft of light that falls on the Beloved Face, so that as in the photograph, you do not think about the light, nor the origin of the light, but you think about the face that it reveals.[1]

In other words, don't glorify the fire; glorify the One whom the fire reveals. Since it is the Holy Spirit's role to exalt Christ in all He does, who are we to take the focus away from Christ and to put it on what the Holy Spirit does?

Jesus Corrects His Disciples

When the disciples returned from one of their short-term mission trips, they got caught up in talking about the manifestations that had occurred. They returned to Jesus slapping high fives and dancing around the fire, recapping stories of demons that had manifested in unusual and bizarre ways: "The seventy-two returned with joy and said, 'Lord, even the demons submit to us in your name'" (Luke 10:17).

Jesus shared their joy and exhilaration: "At that time Jesus [was] full of joy through the Holy Spirit" (10:21). At the same time He corrected the focus of their celebration with a gentle rebuke: "Do not rejoice that the spirits submit to you, but rejoice that your names are written in heaven" (10:20). He was telling His disciples, "Keep the focus on Me—on what *I* do, not what *you* do. Focus on what I do *in* you, not what I do *through* you." Our focus is always to remain on Christ.

Now It's Your Turn: Day 15 Action Step

There is no limit to what God can do through us as long as we give Him all the glory.

Today week three comes to an end, and we celebrate the midway point in our adventure. Today's assignment is simple: give thanks. Using the guidelines below, record the specific works that God has done in you and around you in the lives of others in your church family since the adventure started. "Not to us, O LORD, not to us but to your name be the glory" (Ps. 115:1).

I glorify Christ for specific things that He has done in me: _____
_____

I glorify Christ for what He has taught me about Himself: _____
_____

I glorify Christ for what He has taught me about myself: _____
_____

I glorify Christ for what I have learned about Christ's church: _____
_____

Lord Jesus, what You are teaching me today is _____
_____

Lord Jesus, the action step that I will take is _____
_____

Week 3: Questions for Small Groups

1. Have someone in the group read Acts 2:1–15 aloud. What strikes you about this account?

2. What other examples in the Bible can you think of in which people encountered the manifest presence of God?

3. Describe the manifest presence of God. What are some of the contrasts between the manifest presence and the omnipresence of God?

4. Dream a little. What would it look like for the fullness of Christ to fill your local church? Be specific.

5. Why is it so important to give control to Christ when you are filled with the Holy Spirit? What would it mean for your church family to give your church to God?

6. What does it mean to receive the fullness of the Holy Spirit corporately? As a group, read aloud the model prayer from day fourteen to corporately receive the Holy Spirit. What are your reactions to this prayer?

7. How can you, your nuclear family and your small group pray a prayer like this to corporately receive the fullness of the Holy Spirit?

8. As your small group and church family receive greater fullness of the Holy Spirit, what changes do you expect to see? Be specific.

9. Define the difference between seeking an experience with God and seeking an encounter.

10. Why is it important to keep your focus on Christ rather than on the specific ways He chooses to manifest Himself?

Week 3: Advice for Pastors

This week you have a lot to chew on. Every day this week has had the words "lead pastor" written all over it. Don't fear the fire, pray your hunger, give away control and—the big one—receive corporately! If your church family is going to receive corporately, you and your leadership team must be the ones to corporately lead people to throw open the gates to God. Pray about it. Read and reread the promises of God. Don't submit to pressure from people to move forward, but trust the drawing power of the Holy Spirit to help you relinquish control, receive the fullness of Christ and corporately encounter the manifest presence of Christ. You can trust Him.

In collaboration with your church leadership team, consider drafting a similar document for your entire church—a "we relinquish control of our church" covenant with God declaring your church holy and devoted to God.

If you have chosen to go through this thirty-one-day adventure corporately, it will be helpful for you to begin scheduling in your services one- to two-minute testimonies from your people of specific ways in which they have encountered the manifest presence of Christ during the adventure.

Week Four

STEP INTO THE FIRE

Relax. It's not your job to set your church on fire. In fact, I have news for you—you could not set your church on fire if your life depended on it. It may be your responsibility to pray, lead, teach, preach, evangelize, equip, worship and make disciples, but you can breathe a big sigh of relief. Your list of duties is already long enough. You don't need to add one more thing. Setting your *church on fire* is God's job, not yours. Fire is not what we do; it's what God does.

Fire is what happens when God comes to church. Fire is the manifest presence of Christ in conspicuous, unmistakable, tangible ways. Fire is dramatic answers to specific prayers; healings; convictions of sin; power to overcome bad habits; reconciled marriages; visions, dreams or words from God; being born again; being delivered from an evil spirit; radical obedience to Christ and transformed lives. All these are evidences of the fire of the manifest presence of Christ.

When we work, we work. When we pray, God works.

Day 16

CUP YOUR HANDS

I love upgrades. As a frequent flyer, there is little in life I enjoy more than walking up to the ticket counter and being greeted with, "Hello, Mr. Hartley. You've just been upgraded to business class!" I tell my friends that I don't deserve a business-class upgrade any more than anyone else, but I can assure you that I enjoy them more than anyone!

One of my favorite discoveries as a follower of Christ is that the kingdom of God is full of upgrades. It's true now, and it will be true through all eternity—we will go from fullness to fullness, glory to glory, strength to strength, blessing to blessing. I learned this life-transforming kingdom principle with my wonderful church family in Atlanta.

I Don't Want to Cup My Hands

When I first arrived in Atlanta, I felt overwhelmed by the challenge of pastoring an influential church with such a great history. I was well aware of the fact that I did not have in myself all that I needed to be successful. As I prayed and sought the Lord for His blessing, He kept saying to me, "Cup your hands." No matter where I was, God said the same thing, "Cup your hands." At first I obediently extended my hands in front of me and lifted my empty palms up to the Lord as if I were about to receive a gift. When meeting with the Lord one-on-one early each morning at the beginning of the day, or in my small-group men's prayer early each Tuesday, or at my all-church prayer meeting on Wednesday evening, or at my early Atlanta pastors' prayer group each Thursday, or during Sunday morning worship, or with my wife and kids at family prayer at dinner, the Holy Spirit would always tell me, "Cup your hands."

Initially, it seemed to increase my faith and my level of expectancy, but I really didn't get it. *Why should I cup my hands?* I wondered. After months of cupping my hands, although I now hate to admit it, it began to bug me. God never let up. It was annoying. At times I tried to argue with Him, "I don't want to cup my hands. I don't feel like cupping my hands." He would patiently reply, "Are you praying to receive?"

"Yes, Lord."

"Then cup your hands," He would respond.

He then showed me a thread that runs through the entire Bible. It is the kingdom principle of receiving: "Do not get drunk on wine, which leads to debauchery. Instead, be filled with the Spirit" (Eph. 5:18).

The command "be filled" is a present passive imperative tense. "Be filled" could be more accurately translated "be being filled" or, even better yet, "be in a continual state of receiving an ongoing, perpetual filling." This means that we are never to stop being filled with the Holy Spirit. To put it another way, we are never to stop cupping our hands and never to stop receiving.

The fact is, Jesus taught His disciples to always expect more: "I have much more to say to you, more than you can now bear" (John 16:12). Jesus told us to ask for more: "How much more will your Father in heaven give the Holy Spirit to those who ask him!" (Luke 11:13). Just think of all the categories of blessings to which we have more and more access:

- More grace (see Rom. 5:20)
- More glory (see 2 Cor. 3:18)
- More honor (see Heb. 3:3)
- More love (see Phil. 1:9)
- More fruit (see John 15:2)
- More joy (see Rom. 15:13)
- More rejoicing (see Luke 15:7)
- More praise (see Ps. 71:14)

We are given permission not only to receive more and more from Christ in this life, but we are clearly told that we will receive more and more in heaven as we continually go from glory to glory with ever-increasing glory (see 2 Cor. 3:18). The primary reason that God wants to heal our "receivers" and empower us always to be receiving is that there is always more for us to obtain from the Lord. God is a God who loves to reveal more and more of Himself, who gives us continual upgrades. He has for us new mercies every morning (see Lam. 3:22–23), new songs (see Ps. 96:1), new wine (see Mark 2:22), a new self (see Col. 3:10), new clothing (see Rev. 7:14); in fact, we are told that He makes everything new (see 2 Cor. 5:17; Rev. 21:5).

God made it clear to the leadership at our church that we have enough prayer meetings in Atlanta, but we need more *receiving meetings*. Just consider how many times God tells us to receive:

> Until now you have not asked for anything in my name. Ask and you will *receive*, and your joy will be complete. (John 16:24)

> Let us then approach the throne of grace with confidence, so that we may *receive* mercy and find grace to help us in our time of need. (Heb. 4:16)

> Everyone who asks *receives*. (Luke 11:10)

> To all who *received* him, to those who believed in his name, he gave the right to become children of God. (John 1:12)

I am often asked, "What's the key to the health of your church in Atlanta?" Easy. Our people have good "receivers." In football being a good receiver is called having soft hands—it means that a receiver can catch the ball under extremely difficult circumstances. God wants to activate the receptors of each of our congregations so that we can have soft hands to corporately receive all that He has to download to us.

Gathering the broader church community together in Atlanta is a challenge we have yet to solve. Several years ago, however, I was asked to lead a three-hour prayer gathering hosted at the Salvation Army worship facility inside the Perimeter (the highway separating Atlanta's downtown from the surrounding suburbs) just off I-85. We were pleasantly surprised to see three to five hundred pastors from around the city gather for prayer. After exuberant Christ-encountering worship, God led us in healthy repentance and then intercession focused on stopping drug trafficking. Our wonderful city of Atlanta is one of the largest centers for illegal drugs on the East Coast. As we prayed, there was a deep sense that Christ was hearing and answering prayer. The next day the front page of the *Atlanta Journal Constitution* read in large print, "Largest Drug Bust in Atlanta History." Wow, you wonder if God withholds these large-scale answers to prayer until we are ready to receive together.

The church has developed a bad habit of driving with its foot on the brake. When we seek, we are far too cautious. Nowhere does the Bible warn us to ask cautiously. We need to get our foot off the brake. When we corporately ask, seek and knock, we need to do so with wholehearted, reckless abandon.

Now It's Your Turn: Day 16 Action Step

It's not your job to activate your receptors or the receptors of others around you—only God can do that. It is, however, your responsibility to *ask* God to activate your receptors and the receptors of your church family. Using the verses in this chapter as catalysts for prayer, spend time right now asking Christ to activate your receptors and those of your people.

Lord Jesus, what You are teaching me today is _____

_____

Lord Jesus, the action step that I will take is _____

_____

Day 17

LISTEN WITH EARS TO HEAR

One of the most exciting benefits of *church on fire* is learning to hear the voice of the Holy Spirit. Virtually all the manifestation gifts listed in 1 Corinthians 12 have to do with God speaking to us and manifesting His presence to us in dynamic ways. It is vital that each of us is able to discern a fresh word from the Holy Spirit and to discern His voice.

Five minutes before writing about this topic in this book, I received a phone call from a fellow pastor whom I had not seen for years. "Fred, I just called to tell you that the Holy Spirit has my ear right now more than at any other time in my life." It was thrilling to hear him share his story so enthusiastically. What God is doing in this pastor's life should be the norm for all of us.

Visit James and Ann

One Saturday the Holy Spirit very clearly told me, "Visit James and Ann McKnight." I was at church working on my sermon, so I tried to ignore Him. It had already been a heavy week, and my Sunday morning message, which normally would have been done by Wednesday or Thursday, was still unprepared. My study time was dragging on like a tractor pull. The more I tried, the harder I pulled. My wife and kids were home alone wondering why I wasn't with them, and now God was adding to my load!

Again He said, "Visit James and Ann McKnight."

This time I thought I had better reply. "Can't You see I'm busy, Lord?" I said, but it didn't help.

Unfazed by my appeal, again He told me, "Visit James and Ann McKnight."

I picked up the phone and tried calling James and Ann, but the line was busy. "See, Lord, they must be busy," I argued.

"I didn't tell you to call them," He said emphatically. "I told you to visit James and Ann McKnight."

Realizing that I wasn't getting much sermonizing done anyway and that God must have a good reason for His instructions, I got in my car and drove to the McKnights' home.

Ann was standing in the driveway distraught, waving her arms back and forth. "Oh, Pastor, I'm so glad you're here!" She explained to me that James had just fallen down the stairs and hit his head badly. She was standing in the driveway waiting for the ambulance. The rescue unit arrived within minutes and pronounced James dead of a massive cardiac arrest.

"Pastor, God sent you here to be with me at this time," she stated in her shocked state. "There is no one I needed more than you." I will never forget those words. Then she asked me, "How did you know to come?" I felt like telling her, "God has my number."

The key to following Christ is hearing His voice. Jesus made it very clear, "He goes on ahead of them, and his sheep follow him because they know his voice" (John 10:4). Good listeners make the best followers.

Every year in Scotland there is a sheepdog competition in which the dogs separate the sheep into separate pens. The sheepdogs respond only to the sound of their master's whistle, and the dog that herds the sheep into the separate pens the fastest wins. Last year the owner of the winning dog was asked why his dog had won. "It's quite simple," he explained. "My dog is the best listener."

Paul says, "Those who are led by the Spirit of God are sons of God" (Rom. 8:14). We all have the ability to hear and follow the voice and leadership of the Holy Spirit. For this reason we are told, "Since we live by the Spirit, let us keep in step with the Spirit" (Gal. 5:25).

When Paul was in the upper room with his prophet prayer partners in Antioch, they all heard the same thing: "The Holy Spirit said, 'Set apart for me Barnabas and Saul'" (Acts 13:2). A unique message is given by Christ to each of the seven churches in the book of the Revelation, but there is one statement and only one statement that He makes to all seven churches: "He who has an ear, let him hear what the Spirit says to the churches" (Rev. 2:7, 11, 17, 29; 3:6, 13, 22).

Notice that every church is exhorted to hear, recognize and obey the voice of the Holy Spirit. Why would Jesus give this solitary command to every single church if it were not of preeminent importance to the church today? These words apply to every church through the ages. Some features of individual churches may change, but the one universal constant is the ability of every Christian and every congregation to hear the voice of the Holy Spirit. For this reason the writer of the book of Hebrews says several times, "Today, if you hear his voice, do not harden your hearts" (Heb. 3:7–8, 15; 4:7).

Some have argued about the biblical principle of hearing the Holy Spirit today. They suggest that the complete formation of the Bible stopped the Holy Spirit from speaking to the church other than through the written Word. The Bible is certainly the only complete revelation and absolute authority by which we judge every other word from God. As the great Bible expositor Dr. Lloyd-Jones used to say, "The Bible was not given to replace direct revelation; it was given to correct abuses."[1]

The apostle Paul said precisely the same thing in 1 Corinthians 12 and 14. The church in Corinth was active in the manifestation gifts—some might even say hyperactive. Some of its members exercised legitimate manifestation gifts and others, illegitimate. Some were saying, "Jesus is Lord," and some, as unthinkable as it is, were saying, "Jesus be cursed" (1 Cor. 12:3). Obviously the latter group needed to be confronted as illegitimate, and they were. The fact that some gifts were counterfeit in the church in Corinth did not discredit the legitimate gifts. The apostle Paul never threw the baby out with the bath water. The fact that there were counterfeit gifts validated the fact that there were also genuine gifts.

Now It's Your Turn: Day 17 Action Step

God is always speaking, and He loves to activate our ability to hear. Take three minutes right now and read 1 Samuel 3. What do you learn from Samuel about hearing the voice of God? In your God journal be sure to write down what you hear God saying and where you see Him working. Use Samuel's prayer as you pray now: "Speak, Lord. Your servant is listening."

Lord Jesus, what You are teaching me today is _____

_____

Lord Jesus, the action step that I will take is _____

_____

Day 18

Utilize the Gifts

When our church family learns to recognize the manifest presence of Christ, God will manifest more and more of His presence to us. He does this primarily through what are called the manifestation gifts (see 1 Cor. 12, 14).

As we saw in day seventeen, when Paul and Barnabas gathered with others to minister to the Lord, the Holy Spirit said to them, "Set apart for me Barnabas and Saul for the work to which I have called them" (Acts 13:2). You may be wondering, *How did the Holy Spirit say this to them all? And how did they know that it was the voice of the Holy Spirit?* Undoubtedly, God activated one or more of the revelatory gifts of prophecy, a word of knowledge, a word of wisdom, tongues or interpretation. The Scripture doesn't tell us which gifts were used; all we know is that God spoke to these upper-room disciples by the Holy Spirit.

The Most Disorganized Organized Meeting Ever

I sat in a room full of 260 French-speaking African pastors, where I was to lead a College of Prayer module. The room was full of joyful, Christ-exalting prayer and quite conspicuously full of God's presence. My translator was quietly providing me a running translation of all the Christ-exalting prayer from each corner of the room. The prayer continued in the room, but when my translator stopped translating, my son Stephen, who was sitting at my elbow, whispered in my ear, "Is that what I think it is?"

"I don't know," I whispered back. "What do you think it is?"

"Is that tongues?" he asked.

He was right.

When the message in tongues was finished, I stood up and asked for an interpretation. After a moment of silence, the interpretation came with such bone-crushing conviction that the pastors all fell on their faces in repentance. Men and women began to sob in repentance as they cried out to God for forgiveness. After a full two hours of nonstop repentance, a wave of several messages in tongues and interpretation followed unlike anything I had ever witnessed previously. I did not need to lead anything. I no longer needed to ask for interpretation. The Holy Spirit was in control, and He facilitated the activation of the revelatory gifts faster and more effectively and more encouragingly than anything I could have possibly accomplished.

"You have forsaken Me," one tongue and interpretation said.

"But I have not forsaken you," the next tongue and interpretation replied.

One message was cutting, and the next was healing. God's two-edged sword was active in the room. It was the most disorganized organized meeting I have ever seen. It was a powerful demonstration of the dancing, choreographing hand of the Holy Spirit.

The corporate, God-encountering prayer gathering in my church is called The River. We like that name because it is an intriguing biblical word picture of life, freedom and movement, and at the same time it removes the unnecessary and sometimes unhelpful baggage and associations that come with the name "prayer meeting." Following Christ-exalting worship and prayer in one of our meetings, a woman spoke in an unknown tongue. Our congregation is made up of members from fifty-four nations of the world, and because we encourage all people to pray in their heart language, I don't always immediately recognize prayer in another language as a tongue. This particular tongue, however, was quite unique, and I discerned immediately that it was a message in tongues. As soon as the person was finished, I stood and asked for everyone to be silent and to wait for the interpretation to be given. Within a few moments the interpretation came.

I took time after the interpretation to debrief the experience, to affirm the person and to point out why I was convinced that the word was a legitimate message from God. Several other church leaders affirmed the accuracy of the tongue. No one freaked out. No one broke out in hives or fell over dead. It was a wonderful use of the gift, and it was received as a natural part of the evening and not as a distraction. It added to our God-encountering evening; it did not become an end in itself. This message in tongues not only confirmed many other prayers that had been prayed that evening, but it increased our faith as we continued to encounter Christ.

Discovering the Gifts

There are three distinctly different sets of spiritual gifts mentioned in the Bible:

- *The motivating gifts of Romans 12:6–8.* This group of seven motivational gifts—prophecy, service, teaching, encouragement, giving, leadership and mercy—are given to Christians to build up their fellow believers. Each believer in Christ has one or more of these gifts as a permanent possession, and local churches are strengthened as these gifts are used.

- *The equipping gifts of Ephesians 4:11.* This group of five gifts, or roles, of individual church leaders—apostle, prophet, evangelist, pastor and teacher—are useful to equip the rest of the church for the work of ministry. These gifts are not the permanent possession of the Christian leader but more accurately define the primary role that the leader fulfills. We call them equipping gifts, because the Scripture says explicitly that they are "to equip the saints for the work of ministry" (4:12, RSV).

- *The manifestation gifts of 1 Corinthians 12 and 14.* This group of nine gifts—word of wisdom, word of knowledge, faith, healing, miracles, prophecy, distinguishing spirits, tongues and interpretation of tongues—are occasionally distributed to various church members for the sake of manifesting the miraculous presence of Christ to the believers. The manifestation gifts do not appear to be the permanent possession of an individual believer but rather gifts that are manifested through different believers on different occasions: "To each one the manifestation [or manifestation gift] of the Spirit is given for the common good" (12:7).

The word "manifestation" comes from the Greek word *phanerosis,* which means "to reveal in plain sight or to manifest." The manifestation gifts are always activated in the church family for the singular purpose of manifesting Christ's presence among His people. All gifts build up the body, and certainly to this extent all gifts are Christ-exalting. Not all gifts, however, conspicuously manifest the presence of Christ so immediately among the corporate church gathering as these nine manifestation gifts. For this reason, the apostle Paul clarifies the operation of these gifts:

"If an unbeliever or someone who does not understand comes in while everybody is prophesying, he will be convinced by all that he is a sinner and will be judged by all, and the secrets of his heart will be laid bare. So he will fall down and worship God, exclaiming, "God is really among you!" (1 Cor. 14:24–25). When unbelievers fall down and cry out, "God is really among you!" we can be certain that they have encountered the manifest presence of Christ.

At our church we have discovered many practical benefits of the manifestation gifts functioning properly. While we consider ourselves novices and have much to learn about the function of these gifts, here are a few practical suggestions for their use:

- During our church's corporate prayer gatherings, when someone expresses a need, everyone is encouraged to stay on point and to focus their prayer on this single issue rather than jumping from topic to topic. Corporate prayer functions best when there is continuity on a specific theme.

- We ask people to physically gather around the needy person. It seems that the manifestation gifts function most effectively when standing in close proximity to the person in need.

- We have discovered that while we are praying, God will often communicate through a scripture or a picture. We encourage people to feel free to say, "I see a picture of _____. Does this make sense to you?"

We have also learned when using the manifestation gifts that there is a clear distinction between an initial word or revelation from God and the interpretation and application that follows. The initial word or revelation from God may be given through a revelatory gift such as prophecy, a word of knowledge or a picture, vision or dream. Interpretation relays the meaning of the initial word or revelation. Application is what we are to do with the interpretation. A perfect example is Pharaoh's dream that Joseph interpreted (see Gen. 41). Pharaoh received the initial revelation; Joseph was given both the interpretation and the application.

Just because you may have an initial word from God, do not presume that you necessarily have the interpretation or the application. All these gifts require special Holy Spirit illumination. This is why it says, "To one is given the gift of . . . ." God wants the church family to function in concert with one another. This is sometimes difficult for the alpha-male, type-A pastor to allow the manifestation gifts to freely function. As one who tends to resemble that description, I can honestly say that I have come to love and look forward to the interdependence of the manifestation gifts. I have even learned to sit back and allow others to take leadership when these gifts begin to operate. At times, even though I may have an interpretation, if I sit and wait quietly and patiently for others to step forward, I can enjoy watching the body of Christ function under the dancing, choreographic hand of the Holy Spirit. I am more fulfilled when others are empowered.

Now It's Your Turn: Day 18 Action Step

While you are not the source of the manifestation gifts, and you certainly cannot force them, you are told to earnestly desire the spiritual gifts, especially that you may prophesy (see 1 Cor. 14:1). Take time right now to ask the Holy Spirit to release and activate His manifestation gifts in your life and within your church family. Don't be shy. You can trust Him.

How would you respond to the following questions?

- Is my church family open to welcome and utilize the manifestation gifts? Am I? What do we need to do to move in this direction? What do I need to do?

- Is our corporate prayer gathering conducive to utilizing the manifestation gifts? What do we need to do to move in that direction? What can I do?

Lord Jesus, what You are teaching me today is _____

_____

Lord Jesus, the action step that I will take is _____

_____

Day 19

REPENT AGAIN

If you plan to encounter the manifest presence of Christ, you might as well get used to the fact that you will need to repent. But be encouraged—if the Holy Spirit has led you personally to repentance, He will then empower you to lead others to repentance. It is a kingdom principle that everything Christ has done in you, He can do through you. This is why Jesus told His disciples, "Freely you have received, freely give" (Matt. 10:8).

We need to move beyond the mindset of repentance being a been-there-done-that-got-the-T-shirt activity. Repentance is a gift that keeps on giving. God grants us repentance because He continues to call for repentance. I once heard it said, "I know I have repented because I am still repenting." I don't know who said that, but I like it. When the Bible says, "He is patient with you, not wanting anyone to perish, but everyone to come to repentance" (2 Pet. 3:9), it appears to mean that God wants everyone to come to repentance. Everyone means everyone, including pastors, deacons, small-group leaders, choir members—everyone!

On day three we defined repentance as a complete change of mind, perspective, orientation and motivation. This definition, however, requires a bit more explanation It is helpful to recognize the three essential R's that always accompany repentance in one way or another:

- *Recognize the sin.* No more cover-up or hypocrisy. Identify sin as sin. Expose it to God by confessing it specifically.

- *Renounce the sin.* Utterly reject sin as if spitting out sour milk.

- *Replace the sin.* It is essential in repentance that we not only recognize and renounce our sin but that we go full circle and replace it with what Christ has to impart to us. When Christ fully replaces our sin with His life, we will not go back to our wrong behavior and attitudes.

Eight Hours of Repentance

I was the only white guy in the room full of several hundred African pastors and leaders in Burkina Faso, yet I felt perfectly at home because God was in the room. After giving a brief yet potent message on the anointed Christ, I asked everyone to stand and pray in unison—African style—with everyone praying out loud simultaneously. The place erupted in prayer, sounding like a jet engine, and we sustained a seriously high decibel level for at least fifteen minutes. Then I had everyone remain standing in silence for a full sixty seconds with hands raised to the anointed Christ to listen to what God was saying to the church.

Faces glistened with expectation. Some people trembled. No one moved from where they stood. As we continued to pray, I directed everyone to sit quietly as I asked for a volunteer to share with the group what God had just spoken. Following a time of respectful silence as the group waited for the right person to emerge, an elderly intercessor, affectionately known as Mother Rebecca, motioned modestly for the microphone. I sensed that I could trust her.

She spoke such a timely prophetic word to the church with a spirit of both brokenness and boldness that exposed sin, misuse of money and sexual immorality and also called for repentance. Wow! Everyone in the room, including me, was impressed at the straightforward rebuke and at the accuracy of her words. The room instantly came under bone-crushing conviction. Pastors fell on their faces and cried out to God with loud prayers of repentance, confessing specific sins. Some awkwardly screamed out their prayer as if they were erupting volcanoes whose fire had been pent up deep in their bellies for much too long. Every imaginable sin was confessed. This public repentance lasted for more than an hour. No one wanted to leave, as God was in the house, and His people were responding.

I then asked for another word to be shared. This time I noticed a young man trembling with the fear of God on him. He didn't dare ask for the microphone. His eyes were closed. I could see that God was on him, so I gave him the microphone. As he took it with holy trembling, he spoke a word very similar to that of the first speaker, and yet it cut the entire group even deeper. Those who may have tried to hide during the first wave of repentance now knew that it was safe to come out from hiding. They also knew that they could hide no longer. The first eruption had been small compared to the cosmic blast that now took place. Virtually everyone in the room was weeping before a holy God as they cut loose with their whole heartfelt expressions of sorrow for their sin.

Songs were sung. Prayers were prayed. Bible verses on forgiveness were read. Restoration, grace and mercy filled the room. Before I knew what was happening, six to eight buckets of waters had been placed around the room, and spontaneously people began to wash each other's feet. Smiles, hugs, dancing and joy filled the place. This single prayer service lasted a nonstop ten hours. When I called my wife that evening, I told her that without question it had been one of the greatest days of my life. It was a big taste of heaven on earth. I learned so many significant kingdom principles that day.

We should always give preference to the spirit of contrition. When God comes in repentance, time stands still. We might as well take our watches off and throw them out the window. Our agenda bows to the agenda of God, and repentance is God's trump card. Since the sacrifice that always pleases God is a broken and contrite heart (see Ps. 51:17), who are we to stand up and say, "It's now time to pass the offering plate"? No way. Always give way to the spirit of contrition.

A role that I take seriously is that of leading people in repentance. I have had the privilege of standing in the middle of a room full of hundreds of leaders in full, genuine, God-encountering repentance on hundreds of occasions over the past twenty-five years. Every session of repentance is unique, and every time I stand amazed as I watch the Holy Spirit dismantle defense mechanisms, expose root sin issues, overthrow demonic strongholds and utterly clean house.

High Worship, Deep Repentance

In churches all over the world, our College of Prayer leaders have discovered the kingdom principle that the depth of our repentance is determined by the height of our worship. Let me say this differently: there is a direct correspondence between the holiness of Christ that we encounter in worship and the level of conviction with which our sin is exposed and renounced. It's the principle of "high worship, deep repentance."

When Isaiah saw the Lord high and lifted up, within moments he cried out in conviction and repentance, "Woe to me! . . . I am a man of unclean lips, and I live among a people of unclean lips, and my eyes have seen the King, the LORD Almighty" (Isa. 6:5). When Peter saw firsthand the miraculous catch of fish, he was so broken and convicted of his own shortcomings that he cried out, "Go away from me, Lord; I am a sinful man!" (Luke 5:8). When John the apostle saw the exalted Christ on the Island of Patmos, he fell at his Master's feet like a dead man (see Rev. 1:9–20).

If there was ever a day when you and I needed to lead our churches to genuine repentance, it is today. We need to be able to provide our people with safe places in which they can come clean from years of hidden sin and shame. There is no safer place than the upper-room, God-encountering prayer meeting in which people are ministering to the presence of the Lord.

Only the Holy Spirit can create a safe, antiseptic environment in which deep soul surgery can take place. When the Spirit of God takes the two-edged sword of the Word of God and does bone marrow surgery in the people of God, cutting down to the distinction of soul and spirit where the secret thoughts and hidden motivations of people are meticulously exposed (see Heb. 4:12-13), and yet does this in a safe way that protects people's dignity and restores lives, we know that God is in the house.

Zero Tolerance

It should not be at all surprising to us that one of the most rampant sins we hear confessed is sexual sin. As the great revivalist Martin Luther said, "I have never known a man [or woman] mightily used of God who does not have Jesus Christ as Lord of his sex life."[1] When we are filled with the Holy Spirit, He stamps "Holy to the Lord" in every area of life, including our sexuality, and He stamps "Holy to the Lord" on every organ in our body, including our sex organs. God is calling Christian leaders all over the world to adopt a policy of zero tolerance on pornography.

There is a direct correspondence between a growing pornography habit and a shrinking prayer life. The two practices are mutually exclusive. It is impossible to have both. Pornography is one of the most destructive enemies of the church in North America today. Yet, in a day in which the enemy has vomited an evil, demonic horde on the earth in an effort to pervert the sanctity of human sexuality, our God is raising up a standard of righteousness against him.

Christian therapy groups and support groups, week after week, gather grown Christian men and women who fall in and out of their porn habit, and many tell them that this pattern is normal. It is not normal. It's a cycle that needs to be broken. But we don't need counseling as much as we need repentance. We don't primarily need support, we need deliverance: "If you live according to the sinful nature, you will die; but if by the Spirit you put to death the misdeeds of the body, you will live" (Rom. 8:13). Notice that the key to putting sin to death—including a pornography habit—is the power of the Holy Spirit.

Holy is not the Holy Spirit's first name; it is the dominant attribute of the third person of the triune God. When the Holy Spirit fills us, He stamps "Holy to the Lord" on every cell of our body and in every area of our lives. "May God himself, the God of peace, sanctify you through and through. May your whole spirit, soul and body be kept blameless at the coming of our Lord Jesus Christ" (1 Thess. 5:23).

"Holy" can be a difficult word to understand. The opposite of holy is not evil; the opposite of holy is common, ordinary, generic. To be holy is to be special, chosen, set apart, uncommon, belonging to God. When God looks at us and says, "Holy! You are holy," He instantly sets us apart, and we are special at that moment. When the Holy Spirit fills us and stamps "Holy to the Lord" on our eyelids, we don't see things the same anymore. Our eyes are no longer common; they are holy to the Lord. When we are filled with the Holy Spirit, He stamps "Holy to the Lord" on our hands. From that moment forward the work of our hands is no longer common; it is sacred.

Now It's Your Turn: Day 19 Action Step

If you struggle with pornography, I call you right now to repent. I have great news: Jesus is a Redeemer and will set you free! The sin of pornography involves three evil strongholds—lust, deceit and pride. It starts as lust; then a person deceitfully covers it up and lies about it, and eventually he or she is too proud to deal with it. If you need to remove the problem of pornography from your life, you must deal with these strongholds in their reverse order. First, lay down your pride and humble yourself. Second, stop being deceitful; honestly expose your sin and confess it. Third, Jesus will break the root of lust and set you free. Follow the life-giving pattern of the three Rs of repentance that we saw earlier:

- *Recognize* your sin of pornography. Humble yourself. No more cover-up or hypocrisy. Confess it to God.

- *Renounce* your sin of pornography.
- *Replace* the sin of pornography with purity, freedom, righteousness and integrity.

To fortify your soul, memorize these verses that will help you be an overcomer:

I will walk in my house with blameless heart. I will set before my eyes no vile thing. (Ps. 101:2–3)

The wicked man flees though no one pursues, but the righteous are as bold as a lion. (Prov. 28:1)

He who conceals his sins does not prosper, but whoever confesses and renounces them finds mercy. (28:13)

A wise man attacks the city of the mighty and pulls down the stronghold in which they trust. (21:22)

Lord Jesus, what You are teaching me today is _____

_____

Lord Jesus, the action step that I will take is _____

_____

Day 20

Enjoy True Unity

The intimidating thought, *If I give the Holy Spirit control and welcome the manifest presence of Christ, it may split my church right down the middle* has made cowards of too many of us. Chill out! It is a lie. The opposite is true—when we welcome the manifest presence of Christ, we will for the first time know true, deep, honest unity in our church family as never before.

Be Yourself

In an upper-room prayer gathering, we are more ourselves than anywhere else on earth. We don't have to hide, wear masks or pretend to be anything we are not. All guilt, shame and rejection are gone. The spirit of control, cover-ups, posing and pretense is removed. Bitter jealousy and selfish ambition are history. There is no elbowing, biting, kicking, clawing or climbing over people in the upper room. Instead, there is freedom, honor, respect and, yes, there is love.

Armin Gesswein frequently told me, "The best friends you'll ever have are friends you make at the throne." He was right. The deepest, most lasting friends we ever make are friends we make in the upper-room, God-encountering prayer environment, because this is where we are more ourselves than anyplace else. Just think of it. The upper room is the closest place to heaven on earth. When we get to heaven, we will recognize more people than we ever dreamed possible, because we will be more distinct. The sameness that plagues us here on earth due to fear of man, self-consciousness and social protocol will no longer be active or relevant in heaven. That same blessing that we will all enjoy for all eternity is approximated here on earth in the upper room.

When the College of Prayer held our first meetings in Niamey, Niger, which were sponsored by the mission organization SIM, God came. Pastors who had not spoken with each other for years confessed sin, pride, alienation and competition. Deep and significant reconciliation took place. At the end of the module, the SIM missionary leaders said, "We have been in Niger for twenty years, and the church has split five times.

The College of Prayer is the first ministry that has brought the church back together." We were quick to say it was not the College of Prayer but the manifest presence of Christ that had reconciled the church.

The Invisible Children

Some of the deepest wounds in all humanity are in Gulu, Uganda, the home of the "invisible children." A rebellion force from Gulu called the Lord's Resistance Army (LRA), made up largely of the Acholi tribe, forced children of their tribe to kill their own families and terrorized them by forcing them to join the rebel army. The LRA killed and maimed, not only their own people, but also those of other tribes and became hated among neighboring groups because of their violence, rebellion, looting and ruthless slaughtering of people.

Pastor Mike Plunket, his wife, Lisa, and their wonderful congregation at Risen King just outside New York City led a College of Prayer team to Gulu. Their first one-week mission trip to Gulu was powerful, but the second one-week trip a year later brought bigger dividends than they could have ever imagined. They focused extensively on forgiveness. During one memorable session each person was encouraged to write on a sheet of paper the names of those who had caused them pain and to forgive each one on the list. Then every person tore the list up and walked forward to place the torn pieces on the stage, using the stage as an altar on which to give their hurt and hatred to God. It was a powerful moment.

During the following testimony time, a reconciliation service broke out spontaneously after a woman confessed that she had hated the Acholis because they had killed her husband. As she stood at the microphone and publicly forgave the Acholis, loud wailing and horrifying tears of sorrow arose from all over the large gathering. With one thousand leaders from both the city of Gulu and the neighboring tribal village participating, the tension was high.

Following God-encountering worship and prayer, God came powerfully. At one point, individual leaders from the Acholis stood and asked heartfelt forgiveness from those who had been victimized. Within moments a chilling groan and a collective sob arose from the massive crowd. Then more than a thousand people stood up and asked forgiveness of their violent neighbors for their hatred, bitterness and resentment against them. After three hours of confession of sin, groaning, laments, tears, reconciliation, embracing, forgiveness and love, the group initiated a song in the Acholi language that said, "We repent! We repent!"

We were told later by members of the Ugandan Parliament, "We never thought we would live to see this day. The College of Prayer truly is changing the world." We were again quick to say that it was not the College of Prayer but the manifest presence of Christ that is changing the world, reconciling alienated nations and pouring Christ's redemption into some of the deepest wounds on earth today. After twenty-one years of war, hatred and animosity, God worked a miracle that day of restoration, redemption and reconciliation. Tears streamed down people's faces. The Spirit of God filled the atmosphere.

Unfriendly Fire

As you welcome the advancing rule and reign of Christ's kingdom in your church and in your community, you need to expect to encounter demons. Yes, I said demons. We learn from the life of Christ that encountering evil spirits comes with the territory of seeking God's kingdom: "If I drive out demons by the Spirit of God," Christ said, "then the kingdom of God has come upon you" (Matt. 12:28). Martyn Lloyd-Jones confessed a profound concern over the ignorance in the church of the reality of demon activity: "I am certain that one of the main causes of the ill state of the Church today is the fact that the devil is being forgotten. All is attributed to us; we have all become so psychological in our attitude and thinking. We are ignorant of this great objective fact: the being, the existence of the devil, the adversary, the accuser, and of his 'fiery darts.'"[1]

I could literally share thousands of demon-deliverance stories from Atlanta and from all over the world, but that is not the purpose of this book. We refuse to allow demons to distract us because we know that distraction is one of their strategies. As C.S. Lewis said, "There are two equal and opposite errors into which our race can fall about the devils. One is to disbelieve in their existence. The other is to believe, and to feel an excessive and unhealthy interest in them."[2]

Both extremes are unnecessary. As we welcome the glorious manifest presence of Christ into our church, we will by necessity be evicting evil spirits and tearing down satanic strongholds. Jesus did. Paul did. We will too. The unfriendly fire of demonic opposition is unavoidable as we advance Christ's kingdom.

Right now, in churches all over the world in which the manifest presence of Christ is not being revealed in all His fullness, there are demons irreverently filling the void. These demons are called religious spirits, and they thrive in churches in the absence of God's glory. Any of us who are called to lead in revival and reformation need what is referred to as a "Josiah anointing" to tear down idols, Asherah poles and high places—to kick Satan's butt, so to speak. The apostle Paul knew that one of the easiest ways to unite people is to confront a common enemy: "The God of peace will soon crush Satan under your feet" (Rom. 16:20).

For this reason the Bible tells us corporately to put on the whole armor of God (see Eph. 6:10–18). Every part of the armor corresponds to an aspect of Christ Himself; so when my local church puts on the armor of God, we not only repeat a declaration, but we also do hand gestures that visually correspond to each aspect of the declaration:

> I put on the belt of truth; Jesus is the truth. I put on the breastplate of righteousness; Jesus is my righteousness. I put on the shoes of the gospel of peace; Jesus is the good news. I take up the shield of faith; Jesus is the faithful One. I put on the helmet of salvation; Jesus is my Savior. I take up the sword of the Spirit; Jesus is the Word of God. And I take all prayer; Jesus is my intercessor. I stand complete in Christ, and the evil one cannot touch me.[3]

Now It's Your Turn: Day 20 Action Step

As part of declaring unity in Christ and solidarity with other believers, today is a perfect day for you to put on the armor of God and to make it part of your daily routine as you spend time with God. Do it as a family—your kids will love it! Don't leave home without it. Once you begin putting on the armor and consistently using this declaration, you may even want to do it as a church family.

Lord Jesus, what You are teaching me today is _____

_____

Lord Jesus, the action step that I will take is _____

_____

Week 4: Questions for Small Groups

1. Have someone in your group read John 14:15–18 and 16:5–14 aloud.

2. What are five or more things that we learn about the Person of the Holy Spirit in these verses?

3. What is the primary role of the Holy Spirit? (There may be multiple good answers.)

4. What is the point of cupped hands and receiving that we learned about on day sixteen?

5. In your own words describe the kingdom principle of receiving.

6. Have you ever heard the Holy Spirit speak to you? Share the experience.

7. What are the three distinct varieties of spiritual gifts mentioned in the Bible? Why are we focusing on the manifestation gifts?

8. What would we as a group need to do differently in order to better utilize the manifestation gifts more consistently?

9. What does being holy have to do with the Holy Spirit? Is zero tolerance on pornography a valuable commitment to make?

10. What does evicting Satan have to do with being filled with the Holy Spirit?

Week 4: Advice for Pastors

Expectation without agenda is a healthy perspective on what the manifest presence of Christ looks like corporately. While we know that it is impossible to be inconspicuously filled with the Holy Spirit, we are not the ones who determine how Christ will choose to manifest Himself in our church. It is important for you to continually call your church family to receive all that Christ has for them—not to miss out on anything.

If you have chosen to go through this adventure corporately, it will be helpful for you to select some of your key church leaders who have encountered the manifest presence of Christ in the past three weeks and ask them to share a one- or two-minute testimony during Sunday worship.

Week Five

MENTOR CHURCH LEADERS

Some people think that the centerpiece of civilization is Washington DC, either in the Oval Office or on Capitol Hill. In the country of Jordan, they say that the centerpiece of civilization is the Hashemite Kingdom; in Iran, they say it is the Ayatollah; in Russia, the Kremlin; in England, the Parliament; in Europe, the European Union. The New Testament shows us, however, that the centerpiece of civilization is the upper room, and it is operated from the spiritual axis of power—the throne of God itself. The upper room is the closest we can get to the throne while still on earth.

The strength and stability of your church's upper room is based on Christ's activity in your church family and particularly in your church leaders. For this reason you want to consistently build prayer into your leaders so that they become upper-room disciples. We will focus our energies in week five on the need for training, equipping and empowering those who are the most influential members of your church family.

As your church becomes a praying church that is alive with the presence of Christ, you will experience supernatural unity. The old notion that any charismatic, Holy Spirit influence in your church will be divisive is a bold-faced lie. The truth is, from such an influence your congregation will be more unified than ever before. For this reason this week is vital. While some of this week's content will be geared more toward pastor-leaders who serve within their local church, it is important that everyone within the church family is on the same page. No matter what your role is in the church, everyone in the congregation wants to move in the same direction.

Day 21

Build a Prayer Team

In order to effectively build a praying church, a congregation needs to build a strong prayer team. Obviously, everyone in the church will not serve on the prayer team, but everyone in the church will certainly benefit from the team.

It should be obvious that the prayer team is not responsible to carry out all the work of prayer on behalf of the congregation; rather, it is responsible to mobilize prayer throughout the church family. The first work of every Christian is to pray, but some believers have a distinct calling to pray for their local church and to mobilize prayer.

A strong prayer team is built from a core group of leaders, each of whom has both a heart to pray and a love for the church family. People with both of these callings are needed to form a prayer team.

Jacquie Tyre has both callings. She is one of the best prayer mobilizers I have ever met, and she has a profound love for and loyalty to me and to our local church. God's leading of her and her family to our church was a game changer. She has taken prayer in our church to a whole new level as she has functioned in her sweet spot. God has expanded her territory of influence over the years. She has been the state and regional coordinator for National Strategic Prayer Networks, and she is now the senior leader of CityGate Atlanta, a training center focused on raising up others to fulfill their call and destiny.

So much of where we are today as a local church can be attributed to Jacquie's leadership, anointing and influence of twenty years ago. Jacquie has the virtues and the godly character necessary to work in cooperation with, and in the full support of, a lead pastor—integrity, honesty, honor, loyalty and confidentiality. She has also known the dangers of any form of manipulation or gossip and worked diligently to stop them if and when they ever cropped up. Beyond her Christian character, she has a skill set of leadership, administration and relational intelligence.

Build your prayer team carefully. It is every bit as important as laying a solid foundation for the physical building of your church. A prayer team is made up of five to ten pray-ers, all of whom love Jesus, long for His manifest presence and, preferably, know how to minister in the revelatory and manifestation gifts. They should be people with godly character and maturity who understand lines of authority and confidentiality and who will protect, not undermine, the leadership of the pastor.

There are two sets of people to build the team from: those who have influence with God and those who have influence with people. The first set, those who have influence with God, need to be people who love your church and can express a genuine Holy Spirit call on their lives to intercede for your church. These people are worth their weight in gold. As you look for them, keep in mind a tip that the Holy Spirit taught me a number of years ago: *the shakers and movers in the kingdom of God are not necessarily the shakers and movers in the kingdom of men.* These are the kind of people who will be your prayer force, and they don't necessarily need to have broad influence with people as long as they have significant influence with God.

The second set of people to build your team from is made up of prayer mobilizers. These are the individuals who have influence and leadership among the various people groups in your church family. My church congregation is intergenerational and multicultural, so we intentionally select people for our prayer team who represent the diversity of our church family—men and women, young and old, business owners, laborers and middle management—and we represent as many different nationalities as possible.

The duties of our church's prayer team members are extensive:

- They serve as the leaders of The River, our central, all-church, God-encountering weekly prayer gathering.

- They serve as prayer-ministry team leaders along with our elders during the response time of our Sunday morning corporate worship celebration—praying for people's healing, deliverance, salvation and any other number of needs.

- They make up part of the prayer shield of the lead pastor as personal prayer partners and advisors.

- They mobilize prayer throughout our church life for children, youth, young adults, men and women.

- They facilitate prayerwalks in the neighborhoods around our church campus.

- They help facilitate nights of prayer periodically throughout the year.

- They pray together every Sunday prior to our worship celebration, front and center on the floor of our sanctuary, in a meeting we call Updraft—fifteen minutes of prayer and worship with both our worship team and prayer team. We welcome and minister to the presence of the Lord as people enter.

- Most importantly, our prayer-team members are assigned the highest responsibility to minister to the presence of the Lord. While this responsibility belongs to all of us, at least if no one else does it, then like the Levites, the prayer-team members do.

Just reading this list makes me wonder what in the world I would do if it were not for our prayer team!

As I travel across the United States and from country to country, I love to meet with prayer teams. In my travels and my personal experience I have discovered that intercessors function much more effectively as a team. Lone ranger intercessors can be dangerous. It is much healthier for them to function within a community, like a school of prophets who grow together in grace and godliness. "The spirits of prophets are subject to the control of prophets" (1 Cor. 14:32).

As you finish day twenty-one, you may be thinking, *What does this have to do with me? I'm not part of a prayer team.* Good question. As mentioned earlier, not everyone in the church will serve on the prayer team, but everyone in the church will certainly benefit from one. Jesus is the author and finisher of our faith (see Heb. 12:2). For this reason our prayer life is always growing—never stagnant. As we learned during week one, we want to continue to ask, "Lord, teach us to pray." And as we learned in week four, we always want to pray with cupped hands, going from strength to strength, glory to glory, fullness to fullness.

Now It's Your Turn: Day 21 Action Step

On day nine you began to form your small prayer team with whom you pray. While it may not be your role to form your church-wide prayer team, you can ask God to facilitate the process.

Lord Jesus, what You are teaching me today is _____

_____

Lord Jesus, the action step that I will take is _____

_____

Day 22

Let the Children Come

If our children do not see God dramatically answer specific prayers, we will lose them to Satan. (Please do yourself a favor and reread that sentence.) When I heard those words for the first time, I felt as if the wind had been knocked out of me. As a young father of four great kids, I was suddenly introduced to a whole new world that I had not previously known existed. The instant I heard this statement, it went into my spirit like an injection. I felt its effect then, and I still feel its effect today.

As we build a God-encountering, praying church, we certainly want to teach our children to pray. If our children do not encounter the manifest presence of Christ and develop a passion for Him within their own bellies, our spiritual heritage is only one generation away from extinction. We cannot expect our children to simply be good children; we want them to be God's children, which means that they will have a heart for God. And if they have a heart for God, they need to taste the manifest presence of Christ.

Our children need to do more than simply learn how to punch the right buttons, jump through the right hoops and be involved in outward Christianity that does not ring true on the inside. We need to do more than raise good little bobblehead Christians who know how to nod up and down on cue and spit out correct answers in Sunday school. When kids catch a glimpse of the supernatural power of Christ changing a life, healing a marriage, bringing physical healing, casting out a demon or miraculously answering specific prayers, they will never want to settle for less.

Headaches

God works in sensational ways, but we will rarely discover the reality of His miracle-working power by seeking sensationalism. We don't need to create miracles for God. We simply need to invite Him into our everyday stuff.

When our youngest child, Andrew, was four and at home with Mom all day while the others were at school, Sherry got a terrible headache one afternoon. When she was unable to reach me to ask me to pray for her, she asked Andrew instead. Sitting on the couch next to her, Andrew put his little hand on his mother's shoulder and prayed a simple prayer. Sherry's headache immediately disappeared.

When I got home that evening, Sherry was ecstatic. She told me every detail as Andrew and each of our children listened attentively. You should have seen the look on Andrew's face. He knew that his great, big God had answered his simple, little prayer and worked a miracle in his mother's body. That day he tasted the manifest presence of Christ.

You see, when Andrew was a year old, he'd had a clogged tear duct that always tore. The doctors had told us that it would require sticking a needle into his eye to unclog it. The thought of that needle going into his eyeball had been horrifying, so we'd prayed for him, and God had immediately unclogged the tear duct. We always told Andrew about this miracle. Now when anyone in the family or circle of friends has an illness, Andrew is quick to believe God for healing, because he has experienced it firsthand.

Lord, Teach Us to Pray as Children

As we build a praying church, we want to build praying kids. I have good news: kids love to pray. I have even better news: they are great at prayer! When Jesus said, "Let the little children come to me" (Mark 10:14), He not only opened the door for children, but He was also telling all of us that in order to come to Him, we need to become like little children.

Our church teaches children to pray. Every Sunday during children's church, which we call "Time with Abba," children spend the majority of an hour in worship and prayer.[1] We teach them how to pray Scripture, how to recognize the voice of the Holy Spirit, how to receive visions or pictures from God, how to pray for healing and how to ask for the nations. Our children's workers are very creative and led by the Holy Spirit.

When they pray for the persecuted church, they put on handcuffs. When they pray for the nations, they spread out an enormous twenty-by-thirty-foot canvas with a map of the world painted on it. The kids take off their shoes and stand on the country of the world for which they are praying. Thirty-plus children can stand on the map at one time without stepping on each other's toes.

The Bible says, "One generation will commend your works to another; they will tell of your mighty acts" (Ps. 145:4). God wants every church to experience this reality, and He establishes this as an eternal kingdom principle:

> Let the little children come to me, and do not hinder them, for the kingdom of God belongs to such as these. I tell you the truth, anyone who will not receive the kingdom of God like a little child will never enter it. (Mark 10:14–15)

The tragedy of too many churches today is that they are leading children into entertainment rather than into an encounter with the manifest presence of Christ. Rather than program-driven children's ministry, God is calling us back to presence-driven children's ministry:

Program-Driven Ministry	Presence-Driven Ministry
Teaches the Bible	Teaches the Bible
Provides entertainment	Facilitates encounter
Is high energy	Is high encounter
Meets with each other	Meets with God and each other
Encourages children to watch	Encourages children to worship
Is technology driven	Utilizes technology
Entertains children	Empowers children
Babysits	Spiritually activates
Teaches children to follow rules	Leads children into a relationship with God

One Sunday before I preached, I invited all children fifth grade and younger to come to the front, gather around me and pray for me. It was an incredibly powerful moment. At first the children looked at me with a degree of reservation as if to say, *Are you really going to give us the microphone and allow us to pray out loud in front of everyone in the room?* But I did. I will never forget the prayer the first young boy prayed: "God, we love Pastor Hartley. We want You to bless him, and don't let the devil steal any of his stuff!" To this day I think I got more out of that prayer than most others I've heard.

Now It's Your Turn: Day 22 Action Step

Many of you probably do not have responsibility and authority over children's ministry, so it is not your role to try to implement the principles in this chapter. It is, however, your privilege to pray that the Holy Spirit would come on all the children in your church family. Take five minutes right now and pray the Holy Spirit and the kingdom of God to come forcefully on the children in your nuclear family and in your church family.

Lord Jesus, what You are teaching me today is _____

_____

Lord Jesus, the action step that I will take is _____

_____

Day 23

Empowering the Next Generation

If our children do not see God dramatically answer specific prayers, we will lose them to Satan.

Don't worry; you are not back in the previous chapter. We repeat these words because they make a powerful statement that applies just as much to our high school and college-aged students as it does to our younger children.

The upper room is designed for intergenerational, worship-based, God-encountering prayer: "Your young men will see visions, your old men will dream dreams" (Acts 2:17; see also Joel 2:28–29). This is as intergenerational as it gets! When the Scripture says, "Your sons and daughters will prophesy" (Acts 2:17), it means that the manifestation gifts can operate just as effectively—maybe more effectively—in our young adults than in the rest of us. "Even on my servants, both men and women, I will pour out my Spirit in those days" (2:18). This means that any young adult—middle school student, high school student, college student, young professional—can be just as filled with the Holy Spirit as anyone else.

The Great Awakening that started in Jonathan Edwards' church in Northhampton, Massachusetts, in 1734 started among the young people![1] Many revivals throughout history have started among young people or even children. There is a mighty move of the Holy Spirit taking place today among youth all over the world. God is giving the next generation holy hunger, holy desperation and holy expectation.

Young adults want to pray for more than survival. Frankly, they want to pray for more than revival. They are praying for arrival—the arrival of the manifest presence of Christ! Young adults are sick and tired of dead religion and empty traditions. They want reality. They want a God who works, whose power can be seen and felt. The reason so many young people are giving up on the church is not because of Jesus but because of the lack of Jesus they see in the church. Whether they know it or not, what they want is *church on fire*—church brimming over with the reality of Christ's manifest presence.

I recently spent four days with two hundred sharp Christian graduate school students from all over the Arab world—the brightest and best. They are world changers. They were so hungry for God, zealous for worship, eager to learn, responsive in prayer. One of the greatest blessings of my life is that God has given me the opportunity to empower the next generation. He gives you this blessing as well in your local church.

Prayer Rocks

When God mobilizes prayer among young adults, watch out! All heaven will break loose. A number of years ago, when some young-adult Christians learned that the glitter rock band Kiss was to perform in the Glacier Dome in Traverse City, Michigan, they began praying. Knowing the reports that this band openly called on demons during their concert, the young believers prayed that the concert would not happen. They felt confident in their prayers. They even told their fellow classmates that the concert would be cancelled. They prayed behind the scenes.

On the night of the concert, thousands showed up at the Glacier Dome, including many Christians who were praying against the concert. *Coincidentally* during the warm-up, twenty thousand dollars worth of the band's electronic equipment blew up. After an hour of attempted repairs, the crowd was turned away. No concert. This story vividly demonstrates the truth that prayer rocks.[2]

Prayer mobilizer Dick Eastman tells the story of Mark,[3] a young pastor in Pittsburgh, who notified Dr. Eastman in the spring of 1986 that he felt called to travel through the Soviet Union and pray for the fall of Communism. He did so, and he spent the final days of his trip in Kiev, Ukraine, before meeting up with Dr. Eastman in Poland. For several days Mark sat in the square in Kiev's city center under a statue of Lenin, praying that God would use current events to shake the power of the Soviet government so that doors would open to the gospel.

On April 25, 1986, Mark felt the burden lift, and he went on to Poland, convinced that something was happening that would shake the Soviet Union. The next day the papers all across the world read, "Nuclear Power Plant Explosion in Chernobyl." The 18 billion rubles (equal to $18 billion at the time) spent on the containment and decontamination of the nuclear disaster virtually bankrupted the Soviet Union.[4] The accident also gave impetus to Gorbachev's policy of glasnost, forging closer Soviet-US relations through bioscientific cooperation. Five years later, on December

25, 1991, the Soviet Union was abolished.[5] Only eternity will tell the role that Mark's prayers played in the process.

If you are a student in high school or college, I hope you feel your heart beating faster. God wants to set your prayer life on fire. He wants to use you.

If you are looking at your college years in the rearview mirror of life, God wants you to link arms with the next generation in the upper room.

Now It's Your Turn: Day 23 Action Step

You know high school and college students whom you love. Take time today to pray for the outpouring of the Holy Spirit on them by name. Declare these verses over them as you pray:

> In the last days, God says, I will pour out my Spirit on all people. Your sons and daughters will prophesy, your young men will see visions, your old men will dream dreams. Even on my servants, both men and women, I will pour out my Spirit in those days, and they will prophesy. (Acts 2:17–18)

What can you do today to encourage a young adult? Send an e-mail? Write a note? Adopt one as a prayer partner? Invite three to five into a prayer-mentoring relationship?

Lord Jesus, what You are teaching me today is _____

_____

Lord Jesus, the action step that I will take is _____

_____

Day 24

BUILD A PRAYER SHIELD

Whether you are a pastor or a business person, retired or a student, God wants you to have a prayer shield—a team of prayer partners who are called and committed to pray consistently, and in most cases daily, for you and for the work of Christ to be accomplished through you. It is good for you to communicate your specific needs, challenges and assignments to this group at least once a month. Please read the next statement slowly, carefully and prayerfully:

> If you do not currently have a prayer shield, it is probably because you don't think you need one or because you don't think your assignment is important enough to require one. In either case, you are wrong.

You may be thinking, *Well, I don't need a prayer team. I don't have a high calling like a pastor or a missionary does; they need prayer covering, but I don't.* Not so fast. If you are in Christ, you have a call of God on your life. Don't ever feel inferior or substandard. Every call of God on our lives is a high calling and a supernatural one. For this reason we all need a prayer shield.

The apostle Paul knew that he needed a prayer shield. No less than five distinct times he recruited personal prayer partners to pray for him and for Christ's work through him:

> Brothers, pray for us. (1 Thess. 5:25)

> I urge you, brothers, by our Lord Jesus Christ and by the love of the Spirit, to join me in my struggle by praying to God for me. (Rom. 15:30)

> You help us by your prayers. (2 Cor. 1:11)

> I know that through your prayers and the help given by the Spirit of Jesus Christ, what has happened to me will turn out for my deliverance. (Phil. 1:19)

> I hope to be restored to you in answer to your prayers. (Philem. 22)

I love the emphatic statement that C. Peter Wagner makes encouraging all of us to build a prayer shield:

> I am personally convinced the following statement is true: The most underutilized source of spiritual power in our churches today is intercession for Christian leaders. I purposely did not say "one of the most underutilized sources of power" because I do not believe anything else this important is actually so neglected. We do not do it, and we usually do not even talk about it.[1]

Wagner states that there are three levels of prayer partners that are helpful:[2]

- *Level 3 intercessors*: The casual prayer partner who prays for us when God brings us to that person's mind. How useful these prayer partners are to us is unknown.

- *Level 2 intercessors*: The committed and informed prayer partner who is committed to pray for us consistently, if not daily, and with whom we communicate consistently. These people pray for us with both love and knowledge. If we have twelve-plus of these intercessors, their benefit to us is substantial.

- *Level 1 intercessors*: The qualified, called and appointed prayer partners who have clean hands and a pure heart and do not lift up their souls to an idol (see Ps. 15; 24:3–6). They are qualified to ascend the hill of the Lord and would publicly say that a primary reason that they are alive is to pray for us as their high level assignment from the Lord. These intercessors are few in number, and if we have two or three of these, God has shown us unusual favor.

I love to honor my prayer shield.[3] I give careful thought to consistently and creatively expressing appreciation to those who pray for me and for Christ's work to be accomplished through me. I recruited my first prayer partners when I first went off to college. I sent out letters to many people in my home church asking them to let me know if they would be willing to pray for me daily through my college years. To my surprise eighteen wonderful people agreed. I am confident that the reason God blessed me during the four years of college is largely due to these individuals' faithful prayers.

When I graduated from college, my first job was at Shell Point Village, a Christian retirement center in Southwest Florida. What a joy it was to discover that the church there was full of intercessors, many of whom pray for me to this very day. Today God has given me 348 prayer partners who pray for me virtually every day. Most of them are members of my congregation, and others are from around the world. Wherever I travel God gives me intercessors who have territorial jurisdiction in that country that enables them to pray effectively and with authority in their region. I pray consistently, *Lord, give my intercessors prayer. Give them protection from the enemy, direction in the Holy Spirit and revelation of Christ as You empower them to pray for me.*

The future belongs to the intercessors, and we are all indebted to them for their faithful ministry on our behalf.

Now It's Your Turn: Day 24 Action Step

Earlier we identified two primary reasons that people do not build a prayer shield. Is either of them true of you?

- You don't think you need it.
- You don't think your assignment is important enough to require it.

If either of these reasons has kept you from building a prayer shield, repent. Don't allow pride or an overinflated view of your abilities to keep you from asking people to pray for you. On the other extreme, don't sell yourself or your calling short—your calling, like mine, is a high one. Every calling is a high calling and worthy of recruiting people to pray for it. In the space below write the names of people whom God brings to your mind and whom you could approach this week and recruit to serve as the first members of your prayer shield.

Lord Jesus, what You are teaching me today is _____

_____

Lord Jesus, the action step that I will take is _____

_____

Day 25

MAKING UPPER-ROOM DISCIPLES

Jesus started His public ministry by assembling a handful of 12 disciples, and He culminated His public ministry by assembling a roomful of 120 disciples. He started with a group that certainly had potential, but its members were by no means men of prayer. But by the time He was done with these twelve three years later they were fully developed, upper-room disciples.

If we learn anything from the discipleship model of Christ, we learn that He intentionally built people who not only embraced their mission but who grasped the upper-room model of ministry. They completely understood that their primary assignment was to minister to the presence of the Lord, and they knew that the success of making disciples of all nations was determined by the success of this first assignment.

A Successful African Apostle

Pastor Willy Muyabwa was a successful Christian leader in Africa when I met him. In addition to pastoring a local church in the capital city of Niamey, Niger, he was founder and president of a Bible college, president of the Assembly of God church in Niger, president of the Evangelical Fellowship in Niamey and father of five children. He was a busy man with more than enough to do.

As I preached to a few hundred church leaders in Niamey on the manifest presence of Christ and called them to repentance for busying themselves with lesser things to the neglect of God's glory, Pastor Willy was the first to come forward in humility and repentance. He and dozens of his colleagues repented that day from busyness and prayerlessness. That day the Holy Spirit spoke to Pastor Willy and his wife and called them to realign their lives and establish a whole new set of principles, to seek first Christ and His kingdom and to build a praying church and upper-room, God-encountering disciples.

A few weeks ago I was with Pastor Willy in Rwanda along with seventy-three mighty African leaders who are part of his team, all of whom are making upper-room disciples and planting praying churches across Africa. None of them are paid a penny by the College of Prayer.

In fact, all seventy-three leaders paid part of their own way to attend this equipping conference. They are busy and successful church leaders from dozens of evangelical denominations, but they all share one thing in common: they recognize that their number-one assignment is to minister to the presence of Christ and that the success of their public ministry is 100 percent contingent on their ability to receive assignments two, three, four and so on from the Lord. They are each motivated by a wholehearted zeal to reach the final unreached people on earth before the return of Christ. They are well aware that their only hope of accomplishing such a lofty mission is through a revived church.

Pastor Willy has now planted more than fifty campuses of the College of Prayer all over Africa: in Niger, the Democratic Republic of Congo, Kenya, Sudan, Rwanda, Burundi, the Republic of Congo, Togo and Benin.

Where Do I Start?

Whether we are part of the church leadership or the church membership, our mission is the same: to make disciples. When we set our heart to not only be an upper-room disciple but to make upper-room disciples, we will find that it is easier than we may have thought. We want to follow the Jesus model of SENDS discipleship. SENDS is an acrostic that includes the five critical elements of discipleship that Jesus employed:

S—*Select your core leaders.* "One of those days Jesus went out into the hills to pray, and spent the night praying to God. When morning came, he called his disciples to him and chose twelve of them, whom he also designated apostles" (Luke 6:12–13).

E—*Evangelize together.* "'Come, follow me,' Jesus said, 'and I will make you fishers of men'" (Matt. 4:19). "When Jesus had called the Twelve together, he gave them power and authority to drive out all demons and to cure diseases, and he sent them out to preach the kingdom of God and to heal the sick" (Luke 9:1–2).

N—*Nurture each other.* "As the Father has loved me, so have I loved you. Now remain in my love" (John 15:9).

D—*Divine encounter.* "For where two or three come together in my name, there am I with them" (Matt. 18:20).

S—*Send out your empowered leaders.* "As the Father has sent me, I am sending you" (John 20:21).

This discipleship life-on-life model of ministry that Jesus used is the same model we use in life group and ministry teams in our local church. Everyone in leadership in our church is expected to engage in SENDS discipleship. As we grow, baptize, add members and plant churches, we want to make sure that we are also going deeper and building an increasingly solid foundation. The mistake that many churches make is to put all their energies into numerical growth but never invest in the lives of their leaders. Rather than building lives that build the church, they simply add numbers to the roster. We have found that as we grow in numbers, we need to grow our leaders.

Here's how it works:

- *Select your core leaders.* The most important role that each person in our church has is to pray. Our next most important role is to select the right people with whom to partner and into whom we will invest our lives. We don't want to waste our time. We want to select proven, trusted leaders who demonstrate a love for Christ as well as dependability and then intentionaly and systematically build into them.

- *Evangelize together.* One of the best things we can do for anyone is to show that person how to lead someone to Christ by leading someone to Christ with him or her. I love to lead people to Christ, but I almost feel badly when I do it alone; it is a missed opportunity. We don't learn deer hunting by sitting in front of a TV; we learn it in a deer stand with an experienced hunter.

- *Nurture each other.* The kingdom of God travels along relational lines. The only way to build kingdom leaders is to hang out with kingdom people—to do life together. Hospital visits, breakfast, lunch, ball games, running, golf, neighborhood visits and life group are all things I do anyway, so I try to always do them with my core leaders.

- *Divine encounter.* All life-giving discipleship results in encountering the manifest presence of Christ. Guaranteed. No exceptions. This is the single and ultimate mark of Jesus' method of ministry. For this reason I am always praying with people, laying hands on people, inviting Christ to come into meetings, no matter how large or small. There are few things I enjoy more than meeting with my four governing elders for a finance meeting when an upper-room, God-encountering prayer time breaks out! When you build a praying church, every meeting becomes a prayer meeting.

- *Send out your empowered leaders.* Kingdom people don't just want their name on a role; they want to roll up their sleeves and get in the game. They want responsibility—spheres of influence they can impact. What greater authority is there than kingdom authority, and what greater sphere of influence is there than upper-room, God-encountering disciples?

- God has a group of core leaders with whom He wants you to meet right now.

Now It's Your Turn: Day 25 Action Step

What you decide to do today will determine the long-term success of this thirty-one-day adventure.

- Schedule a twenty-four-hour time slot sometime in the next week or so when you can fast, pray and seek God's face as to whom you will begin to meet with in prayer discipleship. We recommend that you start your fast with an evening meal, then continue through breakfast and lunch the next day. Schedule a date: _____.

- Write down your prospect list of core leaders:

_____   _____

_____   _____

_____   _____

_____   _____

- Draft simple terms for your discipleship gathering, including the date, time of first meeting, frequency of meetings and anticipated completion date. Then invite the people on your list to join you in prayer discipleship. Give the people you invite to join you a two week pray-about-it-and-talk-with-your-spouse-about-it window before they let you know what they will do.

- If you use e-mail initially to send your personalized letter of invitation and your guidelines, be sure to follow up your e-mail with a personal phone call within three days to answer any questions people may have.

Lord Jesus, what You are teaching me today is _____

_____

Lord Jesus, the action step that I will take is _____

_____

Week 5: Questions for Small Groups

1. Have someone in your group read aloud John 20:19–23. What is the context for this upper-room meeting of Jesus and His disciples?

2. Look carefully at each of the five statements Jesus makes in this passage related to SENDS discipleship (we looked at these on day 25). Taking one statement at a time, what is the significance of each one?

3. What do these five statements tell us about the disciples? About Christ? About the upper room?

4. Describe the purpose of a prayer team in the local church. How would your church benefit from such a prayer team? Be specific.

5. Why did Jesus include children so enthusiastically in His ministry? What does this tell us about Christ? About the kingdom of God?

6. How can your group more effectively connect with children? With high school students, college students and young adults? Why is this important?

7. In your own words define a prayer shield. Why does this book make such a big deal about every Christian having a prayer shield? Do you agree with this perspective?

8. In your own words define an upper-room disciple. Give an example of someone you know whom you would call an upper-room disciple. Would you call yourself an upper-room disciple? Why or why not?

9. Explain SENDS discipleship. Does this acrostic accurately summarize Jesus discipleship method? Why is each of the five aspects of Christ discipleship so important?

10.   What would SENDS discipleship look like in your small group? Be specific.

Week 5: Advice for Pastors

This week you will build your church-wide prayer team. When God puts it in your heart to build a praying church, you can be sure that He has already given you the people you need to do it successfully. This means that your prayer team is already within your reach.

Christ will help you identify your prayer team. He will enable you to equip and empower individuals to serve on your prayer team. Make a prospective list of people whom God may be calling to serve on your prayer team:

_____   _____

_____   _____

_____   _____

_____   _____

From the prayer-team duties listed in day twenty-one, which do you think will be most essential to your team? What additional duties might you want to include? What next steps do you need to take to assemble and activate your team?

Based on what we discussed on days twenty-two and twenty-three, you may want to talk with your children's ministry director and your youth workers. Take your time. Ask God about this. Think it through. Pray some more. If you want to gain traction as a praying church, you will want to consider implementing a presence-based children's ministry that teaches children to pray, hear God's voice, confront the enemy and advance Christ's kingdom. Put together a strategic plan to activate your students and young adults in prayer.

Week Six

TAKE THE FIRE TO YOUR NEIGHBORS AND THE NATIONS

Each church, including yours, is designed to have an upper room, and from that upper room God intends to reach your neighbors and the nations through you. This is your final week of this thirty-one-day adventure—week six. This is where everything we've been learning comes together.

If it doesn't impact neighbors and nations, your upper room will not fulfill its God-given purpose. It's time for you to roll up your sleeves. While you are in the act of fulfilling your first assignment—building an upper-room prayer gathering in your church—you want to be fulfilling your next assignment—reaching people around you, both locally and across the world.

Day 26

FOLLOW THE FULLNESS-FULFILLMENT PATTERN

Essentially all prayer means moving toward the vortex of the glory of Christ: encountering the *fullness* of Christ in the church and *fulfilling* the purposes of Christ on earth. Like the two motions of a piston or the two legs on which we walk, the fullness of Christ and the fulfillment of His purposes are the two forces that drive the church forward. We cannot separate them from each other. The fullness-fulfillment pattern is sequential and inclusive.

Fullness is Christ's work in me, and it always comes first. Fulfillment is Christ's work through me, which follows. Jonathan Edwards, the forerunner and key catalyst in America's first Great Awakening in 1740, wrote a book that became a best seller in his day. The title is unusually long yet contains this same fullness-fulfillment principle: *An Humble Attempt to Promote Explicit Agreement and Visible Union of God's People and Extraordinary Prayer of the Revival of Religion* [fullness] *and the Advancement of Christ's Kingdom on Earth* [fulfillment].[1]

David Bryant is a dear friend of mine and a catalyst for Christ-exalting prayer. Notice the fullness-fulfillment pattern he uses: "Spiritual awakening: When the Father wakes us up to see Christ's fullness in new ways, so that together we trust Him, love Him and obey Him in new ways so that we move with Him in new ways for the fulfillment of His global cause."[2]

My African Friends

One of the most thrilling firsthand accounts of the fullness-fulfillment principle dramatically demonstrated in our lifetime is taking place today in Côte d'Ivoire. When one of their denominational presidents, Dr. Celestin Koffi, invited the College of Prayer to work with them, their goal was to become a praying church and a missionary church.[3] They wanted to make disciples and reach the nations.

The amazing thing is that two months after the College of Prayer held our first four-day module in Côte d'Ivoire, the nation fell to a political coup, and both the United Nations and the US State Department forbade any US citizens to travel there. The church in Côte d'Ivoire, however, continued to hold College of Prayer modules twice each year for six years. They told us when we were able to return, "We don't think that the church in Côte d'Ivoire would have survived the civil war if it had not been for the College of Prayer."

When we asked why they felt that the College of Prayer had played such a significant role, they said simply, with tears, "You opened the door to the supernatural but taught us how to avoid excess." Then they implored us, "We now need you to return and train us to do for others what you've done for us."

In 2010 we trained their leaders how to plant other God-encountering, regional upper rooms. They now have eighteen campuses of the College of Prayer training leaders all over the country to be upper-room disciples and to build God-encountering houses of prayer for all nations. In 2014 they had plans to plant fifteen additional campuses.

When the College of Prayer was first invited to serve the church in Côte d'Ivoire, they had a church membership of two hundred and fifty thousand members, and yet they had not sent a single missionary beyond their borders. Seven years later they had more than five hundred thousand members and had sent seventy-two missionaries to countries in Africa. They are now targeting France and Spain. Their leaders would tell you today that this dramatic growth and missionary zeal was the result of God-encountering prayer that led them to encounter the fullness of Christ. The fulfillment of Christ's mission follows the fullness of Christ's manifestation.

Why has the church in Côte d'Ivoire exploded? The answer is simple: they understand the fullness-fulfillment principle. They have experienced the benefit, and they don't want to stop now.

The Fullness-Fulfillment Principle in Scripture

We see the fullness-fulfillment principle throughout Scripture. The first upper room in Jerusalem demonstrates it: first the believers were all filled with the Holy Spirit (see Acts 2:4) and then they began to declare the praises of God to the nations from the north, south, east and west—both Jews and Arabs—with three thousand saved in one day (see Acts 2:5–15, 41). That's what I call fulfillment!

Peter and John demonstrate this as well. When they were released from prison, the believers gathered for prayer only to experience the fullness-fulfillment pattern again (see Acts 4). After they prayed the place where they were meeting was shaken, and they were all filled with the Holy Spirit (fullness) and spoke the word of God boldly (fulfillment) (see 4:31).

The book of Ephesians is a marvelous description of the church, and the entire book is built around this fullness-fulfillment principle. The first half of the book (chapters 1–3) is all about the fullness of Christ; the second half of the book (chapters 4–6) is all about fulfillment.

Fullness	Fulfillment
Christ's work in me	Christ's work through me
Revival in the church	Evangelism in the community
Renewing of believers	Missions to the world
Awakening to Christ	Advancing Christ's kingdom
Dynamic inworking	Dynamic outworking
The initial effect	The resulting effect
Manifestation of Christ to the church	Manifestation of Christ through the church

No one understands the fullness-fulfillment pattern better than Steve Gaines. He knows the vital link between building a praying church and building a soul-winning church. He is currently pastor of Bellevue Baptist Church in Memphis, Tennessee. Prior to serving in that position, Steve pastored First Baptist Church of Gardendale near Birmingham, Alabama. For seven years First Baptist Gardendale led the entire state in baptisms, and they never had an evangelistic program. People always asked what Steve's secret was. He simply explained, "When God comes to church, people get saved." That's what I'm talking about! Pastor Steve Gaines has learned that we don't need to put much energy into evangelism. When we put our energy into attracting the manifest presence of Christ, people get saved.

Now It's Your Turn: Day 26 Action Step

In your own words define *fullness*: _____

_____

In your own words define *fulfillment*: _____

_____

Lord Jesus, what You are teaching me today is _____

_____

Lord Jesus, the action step that I will take is _____

_____

Day 27

GET YOUR ASSIGNMENT STRAIGHT

If we reach our neighbors and the nations, it will not be because of a committee meeting, board meeting or strategic planning meeting; it will be because of a prayer meeting. Contrary to our own popular misconception, our neighborhood and the community around our church are not waiting to see what we and our church can do. People are, however, waiting to see what God can do. It is no coincidence that every missionary journey in the New Testament was launched from the upper-room prayer gathering in Antioch.[1]

Jesus promised His disciples that He would make them successful fishermen: "Come, follow me, . . . and I will make you fishers of men" (Matt. 4:19). With this promise of successful fishing, it is not a mere coincidence that both on the front end of His ministry (see Luke 5:1–11) and on the back end (see John 21:1–11), Jesus provided His disciples with a miraculous catch of fish.

In both cases the men were bone-tired from fishing all night with nothing to show for it, and in both cases Jesus gave them simple instructions: "Don't quit, don't move, don't change course, just slightly alter your approach!" When the disciples secured the miraculous catch at the beginning of Christ's ministry, Jesus simply said, "Put out into deep water, and let down the nets for a catch" (Luke 5:4). The results were overwhelming: "When they had done so, they caught such a large number of fish that their nets began to break. So they signaled their partners in the other boat to come and help them, and they came and filled both boats so full that they began to sink" (5:6-7). For the disciples' miraculous catch at the end of Jesus' earthly ministry, the Lord simply said, "Throw your net on the right side of the boat and you will find some" (John 21:6). What an understatement! Again, the results were absolutely astonishing: "When they did, they were unable to haul the net in because of the large number of fish. . . . It was full of large fish, 153, but even with so many the net was not torn" (21:6, 11). The first half of each of these stories is such a vivid picture of unfruitful efforts in church ministry.

When our best efforts in church ministry come up empty and leave us bone-tired, we tend to think that we need to quit our job, change churches, move across the country or go to work for Home Depot. Not so fast. In both cases, when the disciples were fishing, their location was not the problem—it was simply a matter of timing and approach. Once they heard from Jesus, their nets were quickly filled to overflowing. The point is this: it will only take one word from God for your local church to be packed and to be without enough parking spaces for all the people. The key is getting your assignment straight.

God's Call on You

Not only did every mission journey in the New Testament begin from the upper room in Antioch, but everyone in the Bible who received their life calling received it from an encounter with the manifest presence of Christ. There are no exceptions.

Abraham received his life calling when he encountered God in a word (see Gen. 12:1–3) and later in a vision (see 15:1–21). Jacob received his life calling in encounters with the manifest presence of God on multiple occasions, and he knew exactly what God was asking from him (see 28:10–22; 32:22–32). Moses received his life calling when he encountered the manifest presence of God in the burning bush, and he knew immediately what his assignment was (see Exod. 3–4).

Encountering the manifest presence of Christ is what empowers the church. On Pentecost, as the 120 gathered in God-encountering prayer in the first upper room of Jerusalem, each individual was filled with the Holy Spirit. Those on the street heard the word of God in their own language, and three thousand Jews were saved. Can you imagine seeing three thousand people saved in one day? When the 120 were gathered in the upper room, they were filled with the fullness of Christ. It was the fulfilling Christ in them that brought so many Jews to Christ in a day. When will we learn that when God comes, He can accomplish more in a day than we could accomplish in a lifetime?

The reason that pastors are dropping out of the ministry in unprecedented numbers today is not that they are soft or cowardly—it's that too many of them never received their life calling from an encounter with Christ. Or, if they did, they did not remain in God's manifest presence. It is not coincidental that every missionary journey in the book of Acts was launched from the upper room in Antioch. The missionary movement started in that memorable prayer gathering of prophets who joined Paul and Barnabas to minister to the Lord, which was their first assignment, where they heard from the Holy Spirit that they were to "set apart for me Barnabas and Saul" (Acts 13:2)—their secondary assignment.

Prayerwalking

An underutilized tool that enables us to hear from God and get our assignment straight so that we can rapidly advance Christ's kingdom in our neighborhood is prayerwalking. Essentially, prayerwalking is exactly what it sounds like—praying and walking simultaneously with our eyes open to do two things: worship and welcome. We worship Christ, and we welcome His presence. Steve Hawthorne and Graham Kendrick wrote a wonderful book titled *Prayerwalking—Praying On Site with Insight*.[2] You will enjoy reading it for more insight.

Now It's Your Turn: Day 27 Action Step

Today you have the opportunity to engage in two specific action steps:

- *Call for corporate fasting.* When Barnabas and Saul initially received their assignment in the upper-room, God-encountering prayer gathering in Antioch, they were corporately fasting. This week consider calling your small group to fast for one purpose: to minister to the Lord and receive from Him your marching orders. You want to make sure that you are fishing out of the correct side of the boat.

- *Call for prayerwalks in your community.* Prayerwalking is when you pray on-site with insight. As you walk, worship Christ, welcome His presence and listen to His prompting as you pray with your eyes open.

Lord Jesus, what You are teaching me today is _____

_____

Lord Jesus, the action step that I will take is _____

_____

Day 28

Start with Your Base Camp

God wants every one of us to experience the joy of leading a neighbor to faith in Christ. "'Follow me,' Jesus said, 'and I will make you fishers of men'" (Matt. 4:19). Surely that means that He will give us opportunities to build relational bridges with our neighbors—those who live directly around us in our base camp—that are strong enough to bear the weight of the gospel.

My wife and I got tired of being irrelevant neighbors. We didn't even know our neighbor's names! They could have died and faced eternity without Christ and we would never have done one stinking thing about it. Something needed to change.

One evening in The River, our church's central, God-encountering prayer gathering, those of us gathered started praying for the neighbors who lived within a five-mile radius of our church campus. The more we prayed, the more we came under revitalizing conviction that we needed to do something for these people. Zeal grew. We both laughed and wept in God's presence. That night God spoke clearly to my own heart, "I want you to go out door to door and meet your neighbors." I felt such conviction that I knew this sense was from God, because I hate cold-turkey, door-to-door visitation, and I don't like small talk with people whom I may never see again. I would have never thought of doing such a thing on my own.

It has now been five years since that night. The members of our church and I have now made over twenty thousand door-to-door visits. Prior to our visits, only three people living in a half-mile radius around our facility attended our church on a regular basis, but today several hundred are in our building for some activity each week. When I now walk through the neighborhood, people recognize me and thank me for all that our church does for the neighborhood.

As I walk door to door, I have learned to say, "I would like to pray for you and ask God to bless you. What would you like Jesus to do for you?" I love that question, because it's Jesus-focused and positive. The responses I have received are remarkable.

One man asked me to pray for his wife's new consignment store. The next time I came to his home, he was standing outside with a beer can in his hand talking with three neighbors. "Hey, everybody, come over here," he shouted. "This man knows God. He prayed for my wife's consignment shop a month ago, and today's sales were through the roof! If you need anything from God, you need to ask him to pray for you."

Another time I asked a woman, "What would you like Jesus to do for you?" She broke down sobbing. Her husband had left her that day. We prayed, and God met her. She was in church the next Sunday.

Not every neighborhood is as multiethnic as ours. Our local middle school has children from ninety-one different nations. My local church has members who were born in fifty-four different nations of the world.

The Bible tells us that God oversees not only the migratory patterns of the snow geese but of all people groups on earth: "From one man he made every nation of men, that they should inhabit the whole earth; and he determined the times set for them and the exact places where they should live" (Acts 17:26). The next verse goes on to give the reason that God manages the migration of the peoples of the earth: "God did this so that men would seek him and perhaps reach out for him and find him, though he is not far from each one of us" (Acts 17:27). Here in northeast Atlanta we are discovering that when people move to a new country from other nations, they are more receptive both to genuine hospitality and to the love and the gospel of Christ.

Our Life Group

My wife and I, along with a close friend who lived in our neighborhood, started a life group that meets every week in our subdivision. We printed up simple invitations, distributed them door to door and invited each of our neighbors. Many people have come. One night a new member of our group asked the leaders to pray for him. As we stood next to him to pray, he interrupted: "Now wait a minute. What should I do? No one has ever prayed for me before." Those words were so refreshing. Think of it—no one had ever prayed for this man before. One of the older women in the group said, "Oh, honey, just sit back and enjoy it!" It was the perfect answer. The man didn't need a theological explanation of prayer, as I probably would have given him; he just needed to be put at ease. Since our group started, we have seen eight of our neighbors pray to receive Christ.

The Acts 1:8 model moves from fullness to fulfillment—from the inside out. First we receive fullness—"You will receive power when the Holy Spirit comes on you"—and then we see fulfillment—"You will be my witnesses in Jerusalem, and in all Judea and Samaria, and to the ends of the earth." Notice that the concentric circles of influence start with our neighborhood—Jerusalem—and end up at the ends of the earth:

Jerusalem—our neighbors and those within a five-mile radius of our base camp

Judea—our region

Samaria—those near us who are cross-cultural

The ends of the earth—the nations of the world

Now It's Your Turn: Day 28 Action Step

It's time to start praying for your neighbors by name. If you do not yet know people's names, learning them is a good place to begin. This week go and introduce yourself to some of your neighbors and ask a few appropriate questions:

- "Hi, I'm _____. My spouse is _____. What's your name?" (Write it down. Use it frequently.)

- "We've lived in the neighborhood _____ years. How about you? Where have you lived previously?"

- "I've noticed your dog [your yard, your children]." (Pay your neighbor a sincere compliment on the things you've noticed.)

- "Tell me about your children [or grandchildren]." (Ask about the children's names, interests, etc.)

- "Hey, we want to go out to eat this Friday night. Do you have a restaurant to recommend?"

- "Do you know of a good auto mechanic?"

- "Any special plans for the summer?"

- "We'd love to get to know you better. We're going out Friday night [or having a game night]. Can you join us?"

- "Can I help you with [a domestic duty]?"

- "We pray for our neighbors each week. We want to bless you. Is there anything you'd like Jesus to do for you?"

- "I noticed _____. Is there anything you want to talk about? How can I help?"

Lord Jesus, what You are teaching me today is _____

_____

Lord Jesus, the action step that I will take is _____

_____

Day 29

EMBRACE THE NATIONS

God's plan is to reach a lost world through a revived church. He initiated this pattern from His first upper room in Jerusalem, where He poured out His Holy Spirit on 120 believers. Within hours this small group was miraculously declaring the praises of God in languages they had never learned. Because of the feast of Pentecost, the Jews from the north, south, east and west—from all around the Mediterranean—were providentially gathered in Jerusalem's streets where they heard the gospel for the first time, and three thousand of them were saved in a single day. What a day!

Yet I am among those who believe that the latter glory will be greater than the former glory (see Hag. 2:9). God saves the best for last, and what He is doing in our days and in the final days of history will be even more miraculous and more odds-defying than what He did in the early church.

Some of the Deepest Wounds

My friend Humberto Guzmán is one of the most effective Christian leaders I have ever met. Not only is he a compassionate man, a loving husband and a father, he is also a remarkable leader who leads three hundred churches comprised of seventy thousand members in one of the most dangerous countries on earth: Colombia, South America.

God's hand is on Pastor Guzmán. He serves in a dangerous country listed among the top fifty countries in which the church is persecuted, and he is a target for the drug cartel. In fact, while writing this book, I received word that he was shot with a bullet at point-blank range. Fortunately, he was alert and agile enough to cause the gunman to miss putting a direct hit into his chest. The bullet hit my friend in his arm and went out through the back of his shoulder.

The drug cartels are not pleased with the transformation that is coming to their country as the Holy Spirit empowers the church. Colombia has some of the deepest wounds of humanity anywhere on earth. In many cities in Colombia, essentially everyone has had someone in their family murdered in a drug cartel-related crime. The drug cartels are not afraid of the government, because they know that the government will never stop them. They are aware, however, that there is one force that can stop them: the gospel of our Lord and Savior Jesus Christ.

In 2012 Pastor Guzmán invited the College of Prayer to work with the church in Colombia so that they could become a praying church. His goal was to double the number of people in his churches over the next five years, growing the ministry to include four hundred churches with one hundred and forty thousand members.

Pastor Guzmán knows that this is a BHAG—a big, hairy, audacious goal. The only way it will be fulfilled is if God comes and meets him. Since first inviting us to come help them, he and his leaders have planted seven College of Prayer campuses in one year. Why? He knows the fullness-fulfillment pattern. He wants to reach a lost world through a revived church. He is fully conscious of the fact that the final unreached people on earth will never be reached through a lukewarm church. Never. The final unreached people on earth will only be reached through a revived church. He wants to take his people with him into the upper room so that the Holy Spirit will fill them and thrust them out of the upper room to advance Christ's kingdom throughout Colombia and beyond.

Allow me to tell a story that illustrates how God redeems even the worst of circumstances for His kingdom purposes among the nations. José worked for a drug cartel in the jungles of Colombia. When he contracted malaria, the hospital doctors told him that there was nothing they could do to help him—that he would surely die. Having nowhere else to go, José returned to the drug lab in the jungle and his former friends. They offered him no help and left him to die.

José fell to his knees and cried out in desperation, "God, if You exist, please help me. Make Yourself known to me, and if I live, I will serve You the rest of my life." Suddenly José felt a surge of power run through his body from the top of his head down to his toes. When he stood up, he felt 100 percent normal, and his strength returned immediately.

A few days later he traveled back to the city and stopped at the hospital he'd gone to before for a checkup. They asked, "Who are you?" When he identified himself, the doctors replied, "That is impossible. The José we examined is certainly dead by now."

As he left the hospital and walked down the street, José heard singing in a church, went inside and heard the gospel of the death, burial and resurrection of Christ. That day José remembered the promise he had made to God in the jungle, and he immediately received Jesus Christ as his Lord and Savior. Today he is the pastor of a vibrant church in Madrid,

Spain, and president of the national church of his denomination with seventeen congregations under his leadership.

Now It's Your Turn: Day 29 Action Step

There are nations that God wants you and your church family to impact. List a couple of potential countries you sense God may be inviting you to embrace:

_____

_____

_____

"You will receive power when the Holy Spirit comes on you; and you will be my witnesses in Jerusalem, and in all Judea and Samaria, and to the ends of the earth" (Acts 1:8).

Lord Jesus, what You are teaching me today is _____

_____

Lord Jesus, the action step that I will take is _____

_____

Day 30

ASK FOR THE NATIONS

God wants to build our faith muscle. This is a critical part of our spiritual formation. He not only wants us to want the things He wants, but He wants us to go after them with all our heart. This is part of His maturing process in us. The Christian life is a form of spiritual boot camp in which Christ orchestrates circumstances around us so that God's purposes are always within arm's reach. Then God wants us to just go and fulfill them. The apostle Paul said of himself, "I do not run like a man running aimlessly; I do not fight like a man beating the air. No, I beat my body and make it my slave so that after I have preached to others, I myself will not be disqualified for the prize" (1 Cor. 9:26–27). Then he exhorted the rest of us to "run in such a way as to get the prize" (9:24).

A distorted view of grace teaching tells us that God serves up everything to us on a silver platter, and all we need to do is sit around and wait for the next meal. This may sound logical, but it is not biblical. Of course everything is given to us by God's gracious good favor and by His sovereignty, but He has sovereignly and graciously chosen to involve us in the process of our spiritual growth. He wants us to will what He wills. He wants to harness our wills so that we will invest ourselves in passionately pursuing what He passionately pursues.

This is how Jesus lived. It was said of him, "Zeal for Your house has eaten Me up" (John 2:17, NKJV). This zeal is a fervency and intensity of pursuit that moves us to contend wholeheartedly for a cause.

Ask Me for the Nations

I was sitting in a plane on a tarmac in Africa, waiting for our turn to taxi down the runway. God spoke to me explicitly, "Ask Me for the nations." These words stretched my faith. Even though I was confident that I was hearing the voice of the Holy Spirit, I argued in disbelief, "Ask You for what?" He replied, "Ask Me for the nations."

Then I asked the Lord what I now realize was a ludicrous question, "Is this biblical?" How silly it was of me to ask the Holy Spirit if He was telling me something unbiblical, but this is how I am wired. Instantly the Holy Spirit brought to my mind Psalm 2:8: "Ask of me, and I will make the nations your inheritance, the ends of the earth your possession." Realizing that the context of Psalm 2 is messianic, I asked the Lord for further clarification: "Is it okay for me to pray Psalm 2 when Your Son is the One assigned the task of asking for the nations?"

I will never forget His answer: "What do you think—would I ask you to pray for things that I do not ask My Son to pray for?" I immediately recognized my error. God's word to me suddenly made perfect sense, so I began asking Him, "Give me Israel. Give me Japan and the Philippines. Give me the United States. Give me Canada, Mexico, South Africa, Pakistan, India." The more I asked, the more Holy Spirit joy I felt. "When you get back to Atlanta," the Holy Spirit told me, "I want you to build a give-us-the-nations prayer team." So when I returned home, I began assembling a team of three hundred intercessors to join me in asking for the nations. Today several thousand are part of this prayer team.

When I began asking the Lord for the nations, the College of Prayer had ministry in only four countries; today we are active in over forty nations of the world. We then had 5 campuses of the College of Prayer around the world, and we now have 170 campuses! Closer to home, when I began asking for the nations, we had five countries represented in our local church in Atlanta; today we have members of our local church who were born in fifty-four different nations of the world. I tell my people every Sunday that our church is not a social experiment—it's a miracle!

The Lord of the Harvest

Do you remember the picture of the hourglass that illustrated the immense needs of people at the bottom and the unlimited resources of God at the top with the constriction in the middle representing the pitiful reality of prayerlessness in the church? Jesus lived with this picture in mind. He said, "The harvest is plentiful but the workers are few. Ask the Lord of the harvest, therefore, to send out workers into his harvest field" (Matt. 9:37–38).

Jesus here identified another kingdom principle: the effectiveness of our harvesting depends first on the effectiveness of our asking. God wants us to want it. It almost seems as if Christ withholds some of the greatest kingdom-advancing initiatives until we ask Him about the harvest with a white-hot insistence, a zeal, a determination.

Even after Pentecost the disciples recognized the if-you-want-it-you-need-to-come-get-it kingdom principle. When Peter and John were released from incarceration with a stiff warning from the religious leaders, they could have been intimidated and become passive, but they knew better. They were under higher orders to make disciples of all nations, so they gathered with the believers for God-encountering, nation-discipling, hell-rattling, fear-evicting, witness-emboldening prayer:

> Now, Lord, consider their threats and enable your servants to speak your word with great boldness. Stretch out your hand to heal and perform miraculous signs and wonders through the name of your holy servant Jesus. (Acts 4:29–30)

They explicitly asked for the manifest presence of Christ to embolden their witness. So what happened?

> After they prayed, the place where they were meeting was shaken. And they were all filled with the Holy Spirit and spoke the word of God boldly. (4:31)

I have noticed a ministry principle: when I wholeheartedly ask God to use me to win someone to Christ, within a few days I almost always have the privilege of leading someone to receive the free gift of eternal life. When I recognize that it has been a few weeks since I have led someone to Christ, I realize that this is not normal, so I pray. I ask the Lord of the harvest to stretch out His mighty hand and to use me. Within two or three days—almost without fail—I lead someone to Christ.

No upper room is complete until it reaches the nations. I am quite certain that there is not a single upper-room gathering in the entire book of Acts that doesn't result in soul winning and nation reaching.

Our local church's God-encountering weekly prayer gathering, The River, always follows the fullness-fulfillment pattern. In fact we add another "f"—focus.

- *Focus.* We always start with God-encountering worship as we focus on the exalted Christ. We declare the supremacy of Christ, the excellence of His name and the advancement of His kingdom.

- *Fullness.* We receive a fresh encounter with the love of God in the fullness of the Holy Spirit, allowing people to pray in small prayer clusters of two or three believers, in which needs within the room are met. Christ manifests Himself among us as we give opportunity for everyone to utilize the manifestation gifts as they minister to each other.

- *Fulfillment.* During the final half hour, we normally pray for the advancing of Christ's kingdom, focusing on a particular ministry, city of the world or missional opportunity.

Now It's Your Turn: Day 30 Action Step

Today, begin to systematically and consistently ask for the nations. Don't allow this to be a flash-in-the-pan exercise that fizzles out in a few days. Dig in. Roll up your sleeves. Do some research. Listen to the Holy Spirit as He gives you an assignment of global proportions.

For twenty-one years I prayed daily for the largest unreached people group on earth—the Kurdish people of Turkey and Iraq—thirty million-plus of them with zero known believers during the years I was first praying. I was so overwhelmed by that burden that I couldn't help but pray. Little did anyone know that it would take the Iraq war to open these people to Christ. There are now thousands of Kurdish believers—perhaps tens of thousands. Last year I had the honor of starting a campus of the College of Prayer in an undisclosed location to serve the Kurdish people.

Don't just pray for healing from gallstones and sniffles—there is a world that needs Jesus, and God the Father wants us to ask Him for them. Beyond asking for the nations individually, begin to ask for the nations within your small group. Log on to the College of Prayer website to learn how you can join our "Give Us the Nations" prayer team or utilize other online resources to locate unreached people groups.

Lord Jesus, what You are teaching me today is _____

_____

Lord Jesus, the action step that I will take is _____

_____

Week 6: Questions for Small Groups

1. Have someone in the group read Acts 13:1–3 aloud. What do we learn from these verses about the church? About the Holy Spirit?

2. Where in these verses do we see some of the core kingdom principles that we have learned in our adventure—ministering to the Lord; praying first; receiving assignments one, two and three; following the fullness-fulfillment pattern; others?

3. In your own words define *fullness*. In your own words define *fulfillment*.

4. How would you define your base camp—those within a five-mile radius of your home or your church? From the seven sectors of society—education, finance, government, arts and media, religion, family, science/healthcare—list the ones found in your base camp for which you will begin praying.

5. Using the locations listed in Acts 1:8 as your four parameters of influence, in which area do you personally advance the gospel and the kingdom of Christ? In which does your small group? Your church?

6. Into which of these parameters of influence do you sense the Holy Spirit calling you to become more involved personally? Calling your small group? Your church?

7. Which of your neighbors do you know by name? Which of them do you know well enough to be able to pray personally and insightfully?

8. What specific steps can you take to more effectively build relational bridges with your neighbors as a small group? Pray first and ask God before you start planning.

9. Read Matthew 9:37–38. Take time right now to pray for your neighbors.

10. Read Psalm 2:8. Take time right now to ask for the nations.

Week 6: Advice for Pastors

This week make sense out of this entire thirty-one-day adventure. Things should be getting exciting around your church as people and ministry teams are empowered to sustain an ongoing encounter with the manifest presence of Christ and to extend the gospel beyond themselves.

Consider calling for church-wide fasting and prayer or for church-wide prayerwalking. The benefits will be significant.

You may determine that now is the time to launch your all-church, God-encountering prayer meeting. With church calendars already overloaded, you will have to make some hard choices. Clear your church calendar to give priority to corporate prayer. Schedule your prayer gathering on the best night possible. Strategically name this meeting. Promote it well. Share testimonies during Sunday worship about specific answers to prayers received at your corporate prayer gathering.

If you have chosen to go through this thirty-one-day adventure corporately, take fifteen to twenty-five minutes on Sunday morning to allow your people to share specific ways in which they have encountered the manifest presence of Christ.

Several churches that I know of have chosen to harmonize their outreach ministries under the single title "Acts 1:8 Team," which includes Jerusalem, Judea, Samaria and the ends of the earth. This accomplishes two significant goals: first, it embraces the fullness-fulfillment model, putting the horse (fullness) in front of the cart (fulfillment), and second, it unifies all outreach ministries in the church as one team so that they are all pulling in the same direction rather than against each other. Would this work for your church?

Day 31 and Beyond

DEVOTE YOURSELVES TO PRAYER

Every church prays, but not every church is devoted to prayer. A church that dabbles in prayer is a church that dabbles in the manifest presence of Christ, and a church that dabbles in the manifest presence of Christ has obviously missed the point.

Before Pentecost the early church was devoted to prayer (see Acts 1:14) because it had its sight set on the manifest presence of Christ. After Pentecost the early church was devoted to prayer (see 2:42) because it had tasted the manifest presence of Christ and never wanted to settle for anything else. The leaders of the early church were all devoted to prayer (see 6:4) because they knew that their primary assignment was to sustain the manifest presence of Christ. They refused to dabble. What about you? Have you set your sights on the grand prize of the manifest presence of Christ and therefore refused to dabble in prayer?

Just so we don't dismiss this devoted-to-prayer pattern of the early church, the apostle Paul exhorted the believers in the city of Colosse, "Devote yourselves to prayer, being watchful and thankful" (Col. 4:2). We almost wonder if Paul said these words so that no one would ever think, *That was then, and this is now*, when it comes to being devoted to prayer. It was good for the church in Colosse and it is equally good for us now to be devoted to prayer, not because prayer is an end in itself but because when we are devoted to prayer, we refuse to settle for church life without the manifest presence of Christ.

The word "devoted" is the Greek word *proskartereo*, which is the strongest word in the Greek language for commitment. It means "to adhere, to lock on, to remain steadfastly attentive, to be courageously devoted."[1] Of the ten times this word is used in the New Testament, six times it is used in reference to prayer. It is the picture of a pit bull that sinks its teeth into a hunk of raw beef and refuses to let go or of a heat-seeking missile that locks onto the heat source and refuses to let go until it hits the target. Our problem today is that too many of us take off like rockets and come down like rocks. We don't need any more flash-in-the-pan revivals—what we want is a sustained move of Christ. Consider the distinction between a church that prays and a church devoted to prayer:

A Church that Prays	A Church Devoted to Prayer
Prays about what it does	Does things by prayer
Prays at its convenience	Prays at God's command
Prays when there are problems	Prays when there are opportunities
Has guilt—knows that it should pray more	Has joy—desires to pray more
Announces special time of prayer—some in the church show up	Announces special time of prayer—the church shows up
Asks God to bless what it's doing	Does what God is blessing
Is frustrated by financial shortfall—backs down from projects	Fasts and prays in financial shortfall—receives money and moves ahead
Thinks it is too busy to pray	Knows that it is too busy not to pray
Sees its members as its mission field	Sees the world as its mission field
Does things within its means	Does things beyond its means
Uses God	Used by God[2]

Meet My Buddy Epaphras

After the apostle Paul exhorted the believers in Colosse to be devoted to prayer, he pointed to his buddy Epaphras as exhibit A of what it means to be devoted to prayer: "Epaphras, who is one of you and a servant of Christ Jesus, sends greetings. He is always wrestling in prayer for you, that you may stand firm in all the will of God, mature and fully assured" (Col. 4:12).

It would have been enough for Paul to say, "Epaphras is praying for you," or even, "He is always praying for you," but Paul went so far as to explain, "Epaphras is always wrestling in prayer for you." The word "wrestling" is taken from the Greek word *aganizomai*, from which we get the word "agonize," which means to work so hard as to strain every nerve and muscle. This kind of full-throttle, take-no-prisoners, leave-it-all-on-the-court, wholehearted prayer is the kind with which the early church started, and it is the kind of prayer toward which the church in the twenty-first century is headed.

It is certainly what my church and your church is headed toward.

God wants to deliver me and my church from dabbling, and He wants to deliver you and your church from the same. When it comes to the manifest presence of Christ, we cannot afford to dabble. Christ does not want us lukewarm or tentative, nor does He want us to sporadically encounter Christ's manifest presence. God wants us to seek and receive the manifest presence of Christ as the pit bull grabs its dinner or the heat-seeking missile locks onto the heat source. We want to hit the heat source. We want to hold the course. We want a sustained move of God right down the middle of our church life. We want miracles to be a daily occurrence—physical healings, dramatic conversions, saved marriages, deliverance from substance abuse, visions, dreams, holiness, repentance and the glory of Christ shining with greater clarity than our seventy-two-inch HDTVs.

Meet My Buddy Daniel

I affectionately refer to Daniel Peters as my Navy Seal intercessor. He is my dear friend, trusted confidant, prayer partner and armor bearer.[3] He was born in Ghana, West Africa, and he battles for me like a fierce warrior. As an elder in my church in Atlanta, he and I work closely together on many levels. He frequently and warmly reminds me, "I love you, and there's nothing you can do about it!" Though I've heard it a thousand times, I love it every time he says it.

Daniel prays for me more than anyone I know. At times he prays for me, my family and the work of Christ through me for hours in a day. At times he has prayed for me for eight hours a day, forty hours a week. He fasts for me. He wrestles for me. He has accompanied me on several international trips. I often say, "I get more out of Daniel's prayers than I do out of the prayers of a hundred other people." He is a precious gift of whom I am not worthy. He is a modern-day Epaphras. I share this story with you to illustrate that Epaphrases are alive and well even in the United States.

Yes, there is a growing movement of those who refuse to dabble, who refuse to allow prayer to be just one more activity on their already overloaded schedule, who wrestle in prayer as Jacob wrestled with God. God is today raising up a new Jacob generation: "Such is the generation of those who seek him, who seek your face, O God of Jacob" (Ps. 24:6). What I have discovered about being devoted to prayer like a pit bull or a Navy Seal is that it doesn't come from having an iron will. We don't need to dig deeper or try harder. This kind of prayer doesn't come from an iron will but an empowered will—a will that has been broken, yielded and then trained to obey Christ in the power of the Holy Spirit.

The force of the kingdom of Christ advancing in the power of the Holy Spirit is always out in front of us. God goes first. Always. Jesus set the record straight once and for all when He declared, "From the days of John the Baptist until now, the kingdom of heaven has been forcefully advancing, and forceful men lay hold of it" (Matt. 11:12).

Notice that the kingdom comes on us first—God always goes first. As the kingdom comes on us forcefully, it makes us ever-increasingly forceful in our taking hold of the kingdom of God. This verse in every way describes the church that is devoted to prayer. It's the church that Christ calls for and empowers. It's the church that you and I long for.

Does it describe your church?

Now It's Your Turn: Day 31 Action Step

What are you waiting for? Go for it. You don't need one more action step—you need action. You already have thirty or more tangible steps that you can take to welcome the manifest presence of Christ and to lead others in your church family to do so with you.

Lord Jesus, what You are teaching me today is _____

_____

Lord Jesus, the action step that I will take is _____

_____

NOTES

Day 2

1. Richard F. Lovelace, *Dynamics of Spiritual Life: An Evangelical Theology of Renewal* (Downers Grove, IL: Intervarsity Press, 1979), 82.

2. Moise Guindo served for many years as president of the Christian and Missionary Alliance in Mali, West Africa.

3. I know that this statement sounds like heresy. Of course, God owes no one anything—revival is always a work of God's sovereign grace. But it is, nevertheless, the prayer I prayed. I knew that God was about to do something extraordinary. Perhaps it was a word of knowledge or a prophetic insight, but when I looked into Moise Guindo's face and listened to his words, I knew that I was looking into the heart of God. God was on this man in such a way that I knew that the same God who had brought him to this place of brokenness and desperation was also the God who would use that broken desperation to open the floodgates and pour out His presence on His people. And He did.

Day 3

1. Walter Bauer, *A Greek-English Lexicon of the New Testament*, trans. and ed. William F. Arndt and F. Wilbur Gingrich (Chicago: University of Chicago Press, 1952), 513.

Day 6

1. Jim Cymbala, *Fresh Wind, Fresh Fire: What Happens When God's Spirit Invades the Hearts of His People* (Grand Rapids: Zondervan, 1997), 25.

2. Ibid., 27.

3. Bauer, *A Greek-English Lexicon of the New Testament*, 618.

Day 7

1. Bauer, *A Greek-English Lexicon of the New Testament*, 471.

Day 8

1. Bauer, *A Greek-English Lexicon of the New Testament*, 850.

2. F.F. Bruce, *The Book of the Acts, The New International Commentary on the New Testament*, (Grand Rapids: Eerdmans, 1977), 42.

3. Richard C.H. Lenski, *The Interpretation of the Acts of the Apostles* (Minneapolis: Augsburg Fortress, 1934), 39.

4. Bill Hybels, *Too Busy Not to Pray: Slowing Down to Be with God* (Downers Grove, IL: Intervarsity Press, 2008).

Day 9

1. *Urban Dictionary*, s.v. "Posse," http://www.urbandictionary.com/define.php?term=posse (accessed February 25, 2013).

2. This conversation took place in Lincoln, Nebraska, in May of 1986. This same quote from J. Edwin Orr is recorded in David Bryant's *The Hope At Hand: National and World Revival for the Twenty-First Century* (Grand Rapids: Baker, 1995), 138.

Day 10

1. Bauer, *A Greek-English Lexicon of the New Testament*, 240.

2. In my book *Men and Marriage: What It Really Means to Keep That Promise* (Minneapolis: Bethany, 1994), I wrote an entire chapter on this subject. I also document eleven reasons why husbands break out in hives at the thought of praying with their wives (see page 122).

Day 11

1. Fred A. Hartley III, *God on Fire: Encountering the Manifest Presence of God* (Fort Washington, PA: CLC Publications, 2013), 170.

2. A.W. Tozer, *The Pursuit of God* (Camp Hill, PA: Christian Publications, 1982), 60.

3. Hartley, *God on Fire*, 30.

Day 12

1. Eifion Evans, *Revival Comes to Wales: The Story of the 1859 Revival*

in Wales (Bridgend: Evangelical Press of Wales, 1982), 70; Richard Owen Roberts, *Glory Filled the Land: A Trilogy on the Welsh Revival of 1904–1905* (Wheaton, IL: International Awakening, 1989), 44; Malcolm McDow and Alvin L. Reid, *Firefall: How God Has Shaped History Through Revivals* (Nashville: Broadman & Holman, 1997), 278.

2. Bryant, *The Hope at Hand*, 182–84.

3. Leonard Ravenhill, *Why Revival Tarries* (Minneapolis: Bethany, 1959), 106.

4. Elisabeth Elliot, *Through Gates of Splendor* (Grand Rapids: Harper, 1958), 58–59.

5. Ravenhill, *Why Revival Tarries*, 62.

6. Selwyn Hughes, *Revival: Times of Refreshing* (Farnham, Surrey, UK: Crusade for World Revival, 2004), 13.

7. V. Raymond Edman, *They Found the Secret* (Grand Rapids: Zondervan, 1984), 52.

8. *Smith Wigglesworth Devotional* (New Kensington, PA: Whitaker, 1999), 437.

9. Tim Hughes, "Consuming Fire," *When Silence Falls* (Brentwood, TN: Worship Together Records, 2004).

10. Rend Collective Experiment, "Build Your Kingdom," *Homemade Worship by Handmade People* (Durham, NC: Integrity Music, 2011).

11. Brooke Ligertwood, "Hosanna," *Hillsong Live: Saviour King* (Durham, NC: Integrity, 2007).

12. Will Reagan, "Set a Fire," *Live at the Banks House* (Knoxville, TN: United Pursuit Music, 2010).

13. Kathy Frizzell, Kim Walker-Smith and Nate Ward II, "Show Me Your Glory," *Come Away* (Sacramento, CA: Jesus Culture, 2010).

14. Christy and Nathan Nockels, "A Mighty Fortress," *Life Light Up* (Atlanta: sixstepsrecords, 2009).

15. Matt Crocker, "Fire Fall Down," *Hillsong United: United We Stand* (New York: Sony, 2006).

16. Jeremy Riddle, "Fall Afresh," *The Loft Sessions* (Durham, NC: Integrity/Bethel, 2011).

17. Matt Redman, "Better Is One Day," *Blessed Be Your Name* (Atlanta: sixstepsrecords, 2005).

Day 13

1. Erwin Raphael McManus, *An Unstoppable Force: Daring to Become the Church God Had in Mind* (Orange, CA: Flagship Church Resources, 2001), 176–78.

2. Twenty-five years ago in Atlanta I heard John Hagee say, "Witchcraft is intimidation and manipulation for the sake of domination and control." It stuck with me. I think he's right.

Day 14

1. Lovelace, *Dynamics of Spiritual Life*, 35–39. See also "The Rich Young Ruler . . . Who Said Yes," *Christian History Magazine*, January 1982, 3–4; Andrew Murray, *Key to the Missionary Problem* (Fort Washington, PA: CLC Publications, 1979), 43–86; John R. Weinlick, *Count Zinzendorf: The Story of His Life and Leadership in the Renewed Moravian Church* (Bethlehem, PA: The Moravian Church in America, 1984); A.J. Lewis, *Zinzendorf, The Ecumenical Pioneer* (Philadelphia: Westminster Press, 1962).

Nicholas Ludwig von Zinzendorf was part of a movement known as German Pietism. He was taught and discipled at Halle University by August H. Francke, a Lutheran clergyman and Bible scholar who taught small-group Bible study, national-impact prayer meetings and itinerant evangelism. At nine years old, Francke was so in love with Jesus that he asked his mother for a room that he could use exclusively for prayer.

Francke was mentored by Philipp Spener, who in 1675 wrote the influential revival manifesto *Pia Desideria* (*Pious Desires*) emphasizing the need for repentance, holiness, biblical education, missional advancement and social concern in the context of a vital impartation of the manifest presence of God. Historians, specifically A.J. Lewis in *Zinzendorf, The Ecumenical Pioneer*, have called this work "a Lutheran bolt of lightning."

The contributions of Pietism are far-reaching and include the seven core values of small-group discipleship, prayer groups with a world-evangelism focus, short-term mission teams, Christian hymnology, social action, world missions and Scripture distribution. This stream of German Pietism flowed parallel to that of English Puritanism with its own team of equally impactful leaders such as Laurence Humphrey (1527–1590), president of Magdalen College in Oxford; Thomas Cartwright (1535–1603), professor of theology in Cambridge; Tom Wilcox (1549–1608), a London pastor; William Travers (1548–1635), a Cambridge professor; and John Bunyan (1628–1688), a writer and preacher known for his book *Pilgrim's Progress*. Each of these champions lifted up their voices like a trumpet to call people to a fresh encounter with Christ.

2. Douglas J. Nelson, "The Story of Bishop William J. Seymour and the Azusa Street Revival: A Search for Pentecostal/Charismatic Roots" (doctoral dissertation, University of Birmingham, May 1981), fiche, p. 1–50, 57, 209n116, 197n88.

Day 15

1. Hartley, *Prayer on Fire: What Happens When the Holy Spirit Ignites Your Prayers* (Colorado Springs: NavPress, 2006), 43.

Day 17

1. R.T. Kendall, *The Sensitivity of the Spirit: Learning to Stay in the Flow of God's Direction* (Lake Mary, FL: Charisma, 2002), 37.

Day 19

1. Stephen F. Olford, *The Sanctity of Sex* (New York: Revell, 1963).

Day 20

1. D. Martyn Lloyd-Jones, *The Christian Warfare: An Exposition of Ephesians 6:10–13* (Grand Rapids: Baker, 1976), 292.

2. C.S. Lewis, *The Screwtape Letters* (New York: HarperCollins, 2001), ix.

3. There are many good methods of contending against evil spirits and leading people in practical deliverance from evil strongholds. Neil Anderson has many good resources as does the College of Prayer.

We invite you to check out our website, www.collegeofprayer.org, and to download any number of life-giving free biblical resources.

Day 22

1. If you would like to learn more about "Time with Abba," check out our website at www.lilburn4Jesus.com. You may also want to log onto www.collegeofprayer.org/events/surefire.php and check out SureFire Prayer, a well-developed children's prayer ministry.

Day 23

1. Jonathan Edwards, "A Treatise Concerning Religious Affections, In Three Parts" in *The Works of Jonathan Edwards* (Edinburgh: Banner of Truth Trust, 1976), 1:234.

2. "Intercessors for America" newsletter, January 1976.

3. Dick Eastman, *Love on Its Knees: Make a Difference by Praying for Others* (Grand Rapids: Chosen, 1989), 13–18.

4. "Chernobyl Disaster: Economic and Political Consequences," Wikipedia, http://en.wikipedia.org/wiki/Chernobyl_disaster (accessed March 20, 2014).

5. Mikhail Gorbachev, "Turning Point at Chernobyl," *Project Syndicate*, April 14, 2006, http://www.project-syndicate.org/commentary/turning-point-at-chernobyl (accessed April 30, 2014).

Day 24

1. C. Peter Wagner, *Prayer Shield: How to Intercede for Pastors, Christian Leaders and Others on the Spiritual Frontlines* (Ventura, CA: Regal, 1992), 19.

2. Ibid., 119. Wagner uses different terms but essentially similar categories to the levels of prayer partners listed.

3. Visit www.collegeofprayer.org/resources/free.php to download and print a copy of the "Building Your Prayer Shield" brochure.

Day 26

1. Edward Hickman, ed. *The Works of Jonathan Edwards* (Edinburgh: Banner of Truth Trust, 1976), 279.

2. David Bryant, *With Concerts of Prayer: Christians Join for Spiritual Awakening and World Evangelization* (Ventura, CA: Regal, 1984), 40.

3. Côte d'Ivoire has three major Protestant denominations of which the Christian and Missionary Alliance is one of the oldest and largest.

Day 27

1. See Acts 13:1-3.

2. Steve Hawthorne and Graham Kendrick, *Prayerwalking: Praying On Site with Insight* (Orlando, FL: Creation, 1993).

Day 31

1. Bauer, *A Greek-English Lexicon of the New Testament*, 722.

2. I wrote this contrast a number of years ago showing the difference between a church that prays and a church devoted to prayer. It has been previously published in the College of Prayer's year three curriculum and in several magazine articles.

3. Many church leaders have yet to utilize the wonderful life-giving role of the armor bearer. The concept of the armor bearer is rooted in Scripture in the stories of Elijah and Elisha (see 1 Kings 19:21), David and Jonathan (see 1 Sam. 18:3–4) and Paul and Timothy (see 2 Tim. 2:1–2). The qualities of an armor bearer are passionate love for Christ, desire to pray, loyalty, alertness and a desire to be discipled. The duties of an armor bearer are to pray for the leader (for the leader's protection, direction and revelation), to pray for the vision of the leader, to serve as a personal assistant in order to help as needs arise and to share with the leader what he or she hears God saying.

PUBLICATIONS

Fort Washington, PA 19034

This book is published by CLC Publications, an outreach of CLC
Ministries International. The purpose of CLC is to make evangelical
Christian literature available to all nations so that people may come
to faith and maturity in the Lord Jesus Christ. We hope this book has
been life changing and has enriched your walk with God through the
work of the Holy Spirit. If you would like to know more about CLC,
we invite you to visit our website:

www.clcusa.org

To know more about the remarkable story of the founding of
CLC International we encourage you to read

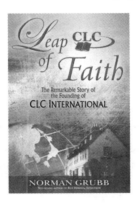

LEAP OF FAITH

Norman Grubb

Paperback
Size 5¹/₄ x 8, Pages 249
ISBN: 978-087508-650-7 - $11.99
ISBN (*e-book*): 978-1-61958-055-8 - $9.99

GOD ON FIRE

Fred A. Hartley III

As believers, we are more alive in the middle of God's white-hot presence than anywhere else on earth. The history of revival is often studied from man's perspective; what we do to encounter God. *God on Fire* explores what God does to encounter us.

Paperback
Size 5 ¼ x 8, Pages 206
ISBN 978-1-61958-012-1 - $14.99
ISBN (*e-book*) 978-1-61958-066-4 - $9.99

LED TO LEAD

Marty Berglund

Led to Lead challenges ministry leaders to grow deeper in faith through lessons drawn from the life of Moses. This book will challenge you to learn from the life of Israel's greatest leader and to move ahead in your own life and ministry, implementing the lessons learned.

Paperback
Size 5¹/₄ x 8, Pages 256
ISBN: 978-1-61958-150-0 - $13.99
ISBN (*e-book*): 978-1-61958-151-7 - $9.99

RUNNING ON EMPTY

Jill Briscoe

Feeling burned out? Unfulfilled? Drained? Jill Briscoe offers hope and comfort for those times in life when we feel empty and tired. With wit and candor, Briscoe draws lessons from several biblical figures that provide spiritual refreshment and renewal to those who are *Running on Empty*.

Paperback
Size 5^1/$_4$ x 8, Pages 176
ISBN: 978-1-61958-080-0 - $12.99
ISBN (*e-book*): 978-1-61958-081-7 - $9.99

This book challenges us to leave casual Christianity behind and take God seriously, just as the prophets did!
Dr. Erwin W. Lutzer, Senior Pastor - The Moody Church, Chicago, IL

Taking God Seriously
Major Lessons from the Minor Prophets

Stuart Briscoe

TAKING GOD SERIOUSLY

Stuart Briscoe

Seasoned pastor Stuart Briscoe examines each of the Minor Prophets, providing both helpful historical context, and demonstrating the relevance of each prophet's message to believers today. If you want to take God's words from the Minor Prophets seriously, this book will help enrich your Bible study.

Paperback
Size 5¹/₄ x 8, Pages 208
ISBN: 978-1-61958-078-7 - $12.99
ISBN (*e-book*): 978-1-61958-079-4 - $9.99

THE PATHWAY TO GOD'S PRESENCE

Tom Elliff

The Pathway to God's Presence encourages those who feel as though they have lost the sense of God's presence in their lives and wish greatly to restore it. Each chapter examines the Old Testament account of Moses and the often-wayward children of Israel, making clear the idea that "there is a distinct difference between God's provision and His presence."

Paperback
Size 4¹/₄ x 7, Pages 144
ISBN: 978-1-61958-156-2 - $9.99
ISBN (*e-book*): 978-1-61958-157-9 - $9.99

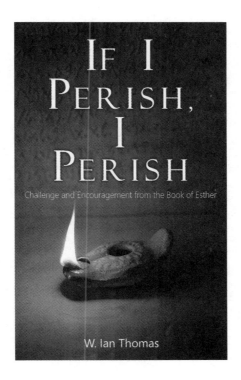

IF I PERISH, I PERISH

W. Ian Thomas

If I Perish, I Perish examines the Christian life through the lens of an allegorical interpretation of the Old Testament book of Esther. The character of Esther, representative of the human spirit, depicts that the call of the Lord Jesus on the Christian is to be crucified with Christ and become alive in the Spirit.

Paperback
Size 4 ¼ x 7, Pages 159
ISBN 978-1-61958-160-9 - $ 9.99
ISBN (*e-book*) 978-1-61958-161-6 - $9.99